A Discovery of Discipleship

Find Jesus Follow Jesus

Bob James

Copyright 2012

Find Jesus Follow Jesus

Forward

WHERE'S Jesus? Isn't that something the world wants to know? Don't you want to know?

Oh, people don't ask for him by name. They, instead, ask, "Where's peace in my life?" "Where's strength for getting through the day." "Where's love? I'm so lonely." "Is there any hope?" "Why can't I just be happy?"

You're always looking for something, someone to fill your life aren't you? You desire the gentle touch of a caring friend, the affirming word from a spouse, or the commitment from a constant friend.

Relationships are a big deal aren't they? Loving relationships make you feel real and full of life. They bring meaning and purpose to who you are. Loving relationships help you rise up each day to say, "Good morning, world, here I am!"

Yes, you want to be loved. And my hope is you'll find the One who loves you forever to know you can have a real relationship him, the Lord Jesus Christ.

Please join me for a walk with Gospel-writer Mark, a young man who discovered Jesus through the eyes of the Apostle Peter. Let's see how Peter and Jesus' other disciples followed Jesus into the homes of sinners, onto stormy seas, before hungry crowds, alongside desperate lepers, and into a new life of incredible wonder and joy.

That's what I hope you experience as you read through Mark's Gospel. I hope you read the scriptures, listen to some of my thoughts, and then pause to consider for yourself their meaning for you.

When you do, I believe the Lord will give you the answer to your questions. Yes, there is only one answer to all your questions. His name is Jesus.

I hope you find Jesus. I hope you follow Jesus. I pray you have a wonderful, eternal relationship with him.

A Good Place to Be

A Good Start

> *Jude 2 Mercy, peace and love be yours in abundance*
> *&*
> *Jude 25 to the only God our Savior be glory, majesty, power and authority*

JUDE begins his short letter with a blessing. I think the blessing is appropriate for each day, but I think it is appropriate as you begin this book. What better thing could happen to you in the reading of God's Word and meditating on its meaning than for you to experience and enjoy an abundance of mercy, peace and love to receive and to give? A life filled with these blessings is a life God honors and a life that honors others (Love God and love your neighbor?)

But there is a problem to live this way, and that problem is essentially the topic of Jude's letter. He speaks of people who are disobedient to God's Word, and those who take grace as a license to do evil. Disobeying God is the reason for strife between people. Seeking your own way instead of God's ways is the reason you do not have mercy, love and peace in your life.

The answer to this problem, of course, is Jesus Christ. That is Jude's encouragement and conclusion to his letter. When you experience God's glory and his power in your life, you will know his majesty reigns over those who denounce and disobey him. When you look to the One who reigns, you will know what mercy, love and peace are. From God you receive these great blessings when you recognize his authority.

Pray for yourself and for others to enjoy these wondrous gifts from God. Give grace, mercy and peace to all around you. You will see what a great difference that makes in your life and theirs.

Pause and Consider: Who is the first person you must offer grace and peace?

Find Jesus Follow Jesus

The Glory of the Lord

> Matthew 2:9-10 *After they had heard the king, they went on their way, and the star they had seen in the east went ahead of them until it stopped over the place where the child was. 10 When they saw the star, they were overjoyed.*

MUCH has been written about the star. Was it a supernova? Was it a comet? Was it visible in the daytime? When did it appear?

How about this idea: The Star of Bethlehem was the Glory of the Lord. God is really good at making his presence known. And he's really good at leading you to where he wants you to go.

Witness the Glory of the Lord in the Hebrews' journey from Egypt to the Promised Land in Numbers 14:14 *And they will tell the inhabitants of this land about it. They have already heard that you, O Lord, are with these people and that you, O Lord, have been seen face to face, that your cloud stays over them, and that you go before them in a pillar of cloud by day and a pillar of fire by night.*

And then on the night of Jesus' birth, see this: Luke 2:9 *An angel of the Lord appeared to them, and the glory of the Lord shone around them, and they were terrified.*

God is light. He begins the creation of the world with light. His light breaks into the darkness of the empty void. His light breaks into the darkness of your empty soul. His light points the way for you to find him. Follow his light and you, too, as the Magi will find Jesus. You'll find joy.

Pause and consider how the Bible is the Glory of the Lord pointing you to God.

A Good Place to Be

Does Jesus Disturb You?

> Matthew 2:3 When King Herod heard this he was disturbed, and all Jerusalem with him.

DISTURBED? Why would Herod and all of Jerusalem be disturbed? After all, the Magi were seeking an infant boy who would one day be a king. The Magi wanted to worship a little boy. Why weren't Herod and Jerusalem excited a future King had been born? Why weren't they joyful the Heavens proclaimed the sign? Why weren't they fired up to find out more?

I don't know. Are you? For years, or perhaps for the first time today you may have heard the good news: *John 3:16-17 "For God so loved the world that he gave his one and only Son, that whoever believes in him shall not perish but have eternal life. 17 For God did not send his Son into the world to condemn the world, but to save the world through him.*

Now I ask, "Does that news get you excited and joyful, or does it disturb you?" How could such Good News disturb you?

Perhaps it threatens your way of life. After all, you like living to your own purposes, doing what you want to do, focusing on yourself, instead of the Good News Giver. Or, it could be that the Good News might cause you to *really live* in Jesus' teachings—how would *that* change your life? Perhaps this is disturbing because beneath the gift of love and salvation lies the promise of condemnation if you do not believe.

The truth is, God desires to disturb you to where you cry out to him, "Save me, Lord! I have sinned, and I need a Savior." Herod and Jerusalem were disturbed because the King threatened their way of life. God wants you to be disturbed because the King promises you a new life.

Pause and consider that the Good News will calm what disturbs your soul.

Find Jesus Follow Jesus

Where's the King?

> Matthew 2:4-7 *When King Herod had called together all the people's chief priests and teachers of the law, he asked them where the Christ was to be born. 5 "In Bethlehem in Judea," they replied, "for this is what the prophet has written: 6 "'But you, Bethlehem, in the land of Judah, are by no means least among the rulers of Judah; for out of you will come a ruler who will be the shepherd of my people Israel.'" 7 Then Herod called the Magi secretly and found out from them the exact time the star had appeared.*

HEAD knowledge was pretty high in Jerusalem. Heart knowledge was very low in Jerusalem.

The Magi told King Herod they had followed a star to find the King of the Jews born in the last year or so. Herod needed to know what the chief priests and teachers of God's Word knew about this king's birthplace. They knew a good deal.

The priests and teachers had God's Word in the scrolls. They knew exactly where the King of the Jews would be born – in Bethlehem. Their head knowledge is big.

But where's their heart? They can see the star. They know more than the Magi. But they're still at home. They're still in their church. They have no heart desire to seek and follow the King.

How about you? You read the Bible. You read these words. You hear God's Word taught. You go to church. But where's your heart? What do you do with what you hear? Does what you know in your mind make any difference in your life?

The teachers and priests missed the King. You don't have to. Go find him and give him your heart. It will change your life.

Pause and consider how Jesus' heart is for you. Is yours for him?

A Good Place to Be

What's In A Gift?

> Matthew 2:11 On coming to the house, they saw the child with his mother Mary, and they bowed down and worshiped him. Then they opened their treasures and presented him with gifts of gold and of incense and of myrrh.

WHAT'S in a gift? It depends on how and why you give it, doesn't it? You can give an expensive diamond. But if you give it with an empty heart, it means nothing to you and little to the recipient. You can give a can of soup with a love in your heart, and it will mean life to the recipient.

The Magi's gifts to the child Jesus were gifts from men who gave their riches from the depth of their heart. They had traveled so long and struggled to find Jesus. They knew from the heavenly sign that Jesus would reign one day. They desired to honor the King. With their bodies bowing down and their hearts full of passion, they gave their best to Jesus.

The thing is, he had given them nothing. They likely expected they would not live to see his reign. They had nothing to gain in their giving. Still, they gave in response to the heavenly signs.

Now, what about you? Jesus has done everything for you. Must I say it? Yes, he's the King of Kings, who reigns over your life because he has died on a stinky cross for you.

Pause and consider...what *will* you give him?

Worship and Obey

> Matthew 2:12 And having been warned in a dream not to go back to Herod, they returned to their country by another route.

THE TIME has come to go home. The journey to Jesus has been completed. The Magi have followed the star. They have listened to the ancient prophecies. These Gentiles, pagan men, have gone to Jesus as God has pointed them to go. Now God points them in one more direction: "Return to your country by another route."

Do you see what happens when you follow God and worship His Son? He protects you and guides you home. If the Magi had returned to Herod, the boy Jesus would have been in danger. The Magi may have been in danger in the presence of this jealous and irrational king. God is protecting His Son. God is protecting the men who came to worship His Son.

Throughout the Bible, God tells you that your only appropriate response to Him is to go to where He is and worship Him. From Abel's sacrifice in Genesis to the power of the elders in John's vision of Revelation, mankind's purpose is to worship the God, who created us.

When you do worship him, Jesus will guide you to a life safe with him, the Savior, for eternity. Worship will lead you to God's presence. Worship Jesus, and the Father will safely lead you to your eternal home.

Pause and consider your journey. Is it to Jesus or not?

A Good Place to Be

Hear

> *Mark 1:1-2 The beginning of the gospel about Jesus Christ, the Son of God. 2 It is written in Isaiah the prophet: "I will send my messenger ahead of you, who will prepare your way"*

WHAT HAPPENS when you want to deliver a clear message to someone? For example, "Dinner's ready!" "It's cold out. Wear your hat." "Our guests are arriving in 5 minutes; set the table."

You get direct with people don't you? Sometimes, maybe you get too direct and express impatience. The thing is, you want to deliver a critical message to someone for their benefit (I hope), and you speak as clearly, directly as possible.

Mark, the gospel writer, has something very important to tell you. He has been around with the Apostles Peter and Paul telling the Good News of Jesus Christ. He's been involved in starting new churches. He knows the key truth to life is this: the gospel of Jesus Christ, the Son of God.

Now he's about to deliver the key truth. Mark's Gospel is short, direct and passionate. He tells you the evidence of Jesus, the Son of God. He shows in words and stories how this is true based on the evidence of Jesus' life.

The first point he makes for the evidence is the prophecy of the prophet Isaiah. To his Jewish audience he speaks directly to say in effect, "Jesus is the Son of God, the one Isaiah, the great prophet, told us would come. Pay attention. Get ready. Respond to the truth."

When you speak directly to someone about the truth, you want them to respond, don't you? Guess what? God has used Mark to speak directly to you. Do you hear? Will you respond?

Pause and consider that the truth will save your life to eternal life.

Find Jesus Follow Jesus

Deliberate God

> *Mark 1:2-4 It is written in Isaiah the prophet: "I will send my messenger ahead of you, who will prepare your way"— 3 "a voice of one calling in the desert, 'Prepare the way for the Lord, make straight paths for him.'" 4 And so John came, baptizing in the desert region and preaching a baptism of repentance for the forgiveness of sins.*

DO YOU like deliberate? I like to be deliberate about my steps each day. Whether they are steps to get lunch, walk off the lunch, take the trash out, or come here to write about God's Word, I want to be deliberate. I don't like to waste motion, time or effort.

You're the same way aren't you? Your days go better when you are purposeful, deliberate in your actions and words.

Do you notice as you read through the Bible how deliberate God is in his plans to bring Jesus to earth? For an estimated 10,000 years from the time of sin' s entrance into the world, God, the Father, has planned to bring God, the Son, into the world to offer salvation to the world.

Now the final steps are at hand. God's deliberate creation and formation of the final prophet John, the Baptist is his last step to make the path straight for Jesus. The deliberate God gives John deliberate steps to take as Jesus' life moves very, very deliberately to bring the ministry of repentance for the forgiveness of sins to the world, to you.

Consider now how God is deliberately offering you these words today. Think of how he deliberately sets you apart to make his path straight to come to you.

Pause and consider what you will do when he arrives at your door.

A Good Place to Be

Fashion Deprived?

> *Mark 1:5-7 The whole Judean countryside and all the people of Jerusalem went out to him. Confessing their sins, they were baptized by him in the Jordan River. 6 John wore clothing made of camel's hair, with a leather belt around his waist, and he ate locusts and wild honey.*

DO YOU like to look good? I do. I'm not trying to say I'm good looking. I'm simply saying that wearing clothes that fit, keeping my hair combed, shaving every day are important things for me. I think most people are that way.

But it appears John the Baptist wasn't. John seems out of sync with even his culture. Why would he dress that way?

Think for a moment of what Jesus says about being a disciple: Mark 8:34 *"If anyone would come after me, he must deny himself and take up his cross and follow me."*

In John's way of living, he was demonstrating what is required of a new spiritual life in Jesus Christ. Jesus and the New Testament writers talk often of denying the things of the world in order to more fully wear the "clothes" of Jesus' desires for you. Mark certainly denied himself. He gave up a comfortable life at home for the discomfort of living in new cultures and in danger of persecution.

In order to live in Jesus, the Apostle Paul writes: Ephesians 4:22-24 *You were taught, with regard to your former way of life, to put off your old self, which is being corrupted by its deceitful desires; 23 to be made new in the attitude of your minds; 24 and to put on the new self, created to be like God in true righteousness and holiness.*

God had anointed John to live apart from the world because he would point to Jesus. Dress up in Jesus. Clothe yourself in his salvation and his majesty. And you'll really, really look good.

Pause and consider it is essential you make the Gospel your fashion statement.

Find Jesus Follow Jesus

Holy Spirit, the Baptizer

> Mark 1:8-9 "I baptize you with water, but he will baptize you with the Holy Spirit."

JOHN the Baptist or "Baptizer" is called so because he focused his ministry on calling people to declare their repentance to God through the form of water being poured over them or being briefly submerged in a body of water such as the Jordan River. Baptism has its roots in the Old Testament as God moved his people "through the waters" of the Red Sea to escape Egypt's army. Later in the desert, God's law required the priests to do a ceremonial washing prior to their entering the Tabernacle. Water washing was a sign of moving from the old to the new.

Now John knows the water baptism is a sign of God's next step in purifying his people, cleansing their sins. God is about to send his Messiah, the Christ, and he will baptize in the power of the Holy Spirit.

The Spirit's baptism will be more powerful—it will be eternal. When the Spirit of God comes upon people, he will awaken them to the truth that they are sinners. He will awaken them to a desire to repent of their sins. He will awaken them to the truth of Jesus Christ.

Spirit baptism is not a liquid washing of water, but it is a spiritual washing of the blood of Christ over you. Yes, it is Jesus, *"who loves us and has freed us from our sins by his blood"* (Rev 1:5).

As you call Jesus "Lord and Savior" know the Holy Spirit has baptized you to that truth. If you are yet to make that faith statement, pray and ask the Holy Spirit to baptize you with the truth of Jesus Christ, that you too, may be saved.

Pause and consider the work of God to save your life to have life with him.

A Good Place to Be

Heaven Tears Open

> *Mark 1:10-11 as Jesus was coming up out of the water, he saw heaven being torn open and the Spirit descending on him like a dove.*

AS JESUS, the Son of God, comes out of the water, he sees "heaven torn open" What does that mean? It is this: God has drawn back the curtain to reveal God to the world.

Here is Genesis 1:3 *And God said, "Let there be light," and there was light.* Here is Isaiah 64:1 *Oh, that you would burst from the heavens and come down! How the mountains would quake in your presence!*

Here is Revelation 1:7 *Look, he is coming with the clouds, and every eye will see him, even those who pierced him; and all the peoples of the earth will mourn because of him. So shall it be! Amen.*

Here comes the light into the darkness. Here comes the majesty of God into his creation. Here comes the holiness of God to remove the sin of the world. Here comes the power of God to overcome even the great enemy "Death".

The heavens torn open is God saying, "My Kingdom has come! My will is now to be done on earth as it is in heaven." The Spirit of God anoints the Son of God to do the will of God in the power of God.

And so he does. Jesus heals the sick, preaches the Good News, dies on the Cross, rises from the dead, and ascends to Heaven. Heaven has been torn open. Jesus has come to seek, to serve and to save you.

Pause and consider that Jesus' testimony of life eternal is for your life.

The Father's Blessing

> Mark 1:11 *And a voice came from heaven: "You are my Son, whom I love; with you I am well pleased."*

TWO very important things happen with these words from God the Father to Jesus, the Son of God. God affirms his Son's identity. And God affirms his Son's value.

Throughout the Gospels, wherever Jesus goes, people want to know, "Where did he get such knowledge?" "Who is this man?" "Who is he that even the winds obey him?" "Who is he that drives out demons?"

"Who is he?" indeed. God made it plain that day. God made it plain later in Jesus ministry in the transfiguration before James, John and Peter (Mark 9). God made it clear when the earth quaked, the temple veil tore, the darkness came, and the dead raised on that awful day of Jesus' death.

Who is Jesus? God made it clear on the day of his resurrection: *John 20:18 Mary Magdalene went to the disciples with the news: "I have seen the Lord!"*

From the prophets, to the Jordan River, to the cross, to the empty tomb, to heaven's throne and one day on the clouds of glory, God has and will make plain that Jesus is the living Son of God. Jesus is the Savior of the world. Jesus died on a cross for the cleansing of your sins. Jesus will come again to reign in glory forever.

Pause and consider: do you see the Son before you?

A Good Place to Be

Tough Start

> *Mark 1:12-13 At once the Spirit sent him out into the desert, 13 and he was in the desert forty days, being tempted by Satan. He was with the wild animals, and angels attended him.*

PERHAPS you've begun a new job or graduated from long years of study. You were excited and feeling well-prepared for the work. Maybe you prepared for years to begin a business. Now the time had arrived. You were sure you could handle any challenge that might come your way. But something happened. You faced difficulties far beyond what you had foreseen. You didn't realize things would be *that* difficult! What to do?

One of the many things that amaze me about this scripture is this: The Holy Spirit of God has just anointed the Son of God to do the work of God in the world. And it seems his first task is to confront the devil. Right out of the chute, so to speak, Jesus goes from his anointing to ministry to a very severe test of his anointing. He faces horrible, unbelievable physical deprivation. Other Gospels record he was in the desert 40 days with no food or water. No mere mortal could survive that kind of physical punishment.

No mere mortal soul could survive the devil's persistent temptations. Jesus faced a most severe test on who he was and what he was to do. The devil was desperate to dissuade him. In the power of God, Jesus withstood the test. He resisted evil. He stood on the truth of the Word of God (after all, he is the "Word become flesh"), and he left the test strengthened to do his work.

This same power is available for you. Where are your struggles and temptations? Go to the Word of God and find your strength. Call on the Spirit, and he will refresh you. You will resist the unexpected hard times. You will overcome through he who overcomes.

Pause and consider how the devil keeps pursuing you and you must keep pursuing the Word of God.

Find Jesus Follow Jesus

Good News?

> Mark 1:14-16 *After John was put in prison, Jesus went into Galilee, proclaiming the good news of God. 15 "The time has come," he said. "The kingdom of God is near. Repent and believe the good news!"*

DO YOU see anything odd here? How does it strike you that "John was put in prison…and Jesus went proclaiming the good news of God."

God created John to point God's people to Jesus. He baptized Jesus as Jesus began his mission. John has clearly fulfilled the purpose of his life.

So this is how you reward people, Jesus? You put John, your faithful servant, in prison where Herod will have him beheaded? Why would you do that, Jesus?

What do you think? Seems unfair, even disdainful, doesn't it? Pause and consider other things Jesus knew. He knew John's future was a heavenly future. Eternal reward awaited this faithful servant. Jesus knew that his faithful preaching of the Good News of God lead him to a brutal death.

The lesson here is that when God calls you to be a Good News giver, you could (likely will) face many challenges. You could be socially cast "in jail", shut off from your friends and family. And in certain parts of the world, you could be killed.

The thing is, as a Good News giver, you are never alone. As a Good News giver, you never die because the Good News is: (John 11:25) *"I am the resurrection and the life. He who believes in me will live, even though he dies"*

Seeing your life as limited to your earthly existence, you may often say, "it's not fair, Lord!"

Seeing your life as eternal in the hands of Jesus you will say, (Luke 22:42) *"yet not my will, but yours be done."*

Pause and consider that Jesus suffered and died so you may rejoice and live.

A Good Place to Be

An Amazing Invitation

> *Mark 1:17-20 "Come, follow me," Jesus said, "and I will make you fishers of men." 18 At once they left their nets and followed him. 19 When he had gone a little farther, he saw James son of Zebedee and his brother John in a boat, preparing their nets. 20 Without delay he called them, and they left their father Zebedee in the boat with the hired men and followed him.*

HAVE YOU ever wondered what made these fishermen and other men leave what they were doing to follow Jesus? After all, they left their jobs, their way of life, their parents, their friends and responded to Jesus' invitation to "Come, follow me." To me, this is an amazing, devoted response to Jesus.   Actually, what is really amazing is Jesus' call on their lives. The culture of the day was that young men who were interested in learning more of God and God's Word would have to go to a rabbi and say, "Could I please be your disciple?" And usually they were rejected because they weren't smart enough, or the rabbi had some prejudice against them.

Not Jesus. He's God in the flesh. God has a plan to save the world from sin. In his love, it is *his choice* to come to earth. In his love it is *his choice* to choose people to be his disciples. In his love, he will take all who drop "their nets" and follow him.

This is a most amazing thing, isn't it?

Pause and consider your response to Jesus' invitation. What must you drop to follow him?

Find Jesus Follow Jesus

Something's Different

> *Mark 1:21-22 They went to Capernaum, and when the Sabbath came, Jesus went into the synagogue and began to teach. 22 The people were amazed at his teaching, because he taught them as one who had authority, not as the teachers of the law.*

HAVE YOU ever been in the presence of someone who really knows what she's talking about? She exudes authority in her knowledge. And her way of speaking assures you she has a mastery of her facts.

When Scriptures says Jesus taught as one "who had authority", it is apparent people were confident of his knowledge. They knew he had a mastery of his topic. And, in fact, one of the terms used to address him was "Master". The Gospel writer Luke uses this several times to record the disciples addressing Jesus.

But there's something more, much more to Jesus' authority than his words. Jesus made it clear he had authority, he had mastery, over disease, over the winds, over the demons and over sin. Jesus demonstrated his authority also in the way he taught the Law of Moses, turning it from a legalistic code the Jews had made it to be into God's saving pattern.

Jesus' authority of the Scriptures brought the reality of God's love to his people. His authority came from the throne of heaven in the power of the Spirit, and the Spirit moved to touch the hearts of men and women who heard the Master's words.

Pause and consider how life-giving the words of Scripture are when you turn your life to the authority of God's Word.

A Good Place to Be

Be Quiet and Go!

> Mark 1:23-25 *Just then a man in their synagogue who was possessed by an evil spirit cried out,* 24 *"What do you want with us, Jesus of Nazareth? Have you come to destroy us? I know who you are — the Holy One of God!"* 25 *"Be quiet!" said Jesus sternly. "Come out of him!"* 26 *The evil spirit shook the man violently and came out of him with a shriek.*

THE THING YOU must know is that evil spirits are active in the world. And they do "possess" – live in and control the actions of – some people. And they attempt to influence the actions of all. I have heard testimonies from people who have experienced demonic possession. They share how these demons spoke to them and turned them to evil actions. They were released from the evil when they accepted Jesus as their Lord and Savior.

Jesus, the Holy One, wars against the evil that possesses and tempts his people. When he tells the demon, "Be quiet." he rejects the voice of evil. In this exchange, you see it is the power of God that removes the power of sin literally from this man. As the demon leaves, it causes the man to convulse.

Demonic possession and influences cause convulsion in the soul, heart and mind to keep you from Jesus. The battle rages each day. Each day you must call upon the power of Jesus Christ, to protect you and free you for victory in the battle.

Jesus is the victor. He stands triumphant on the throne of heaven. Listen to his voice only.

Pause and consider how constantly the Holy Spirit is available to give you power to resist evil.

Find Jesus Follow Jesus

Why Wouldn't They Be?

> Mark 1:27-32 *The people were all so amazed that they asked each other, "What is this? A new teaching — and with authority! He even gives orders to evil spirits and they obey him." 28 News about him spread quickly over the whole region of Galilee. 29 As soon as they left the synagogue, they went with James and John to the home of Simon and Andrew. 30 Simon's mother-in-law was in bed with a fever, and they told Jesus about her. 31 So he went to her, took her hand and helped her up. The fever left her and she began to wait on them. 32 That evening after sunset the people brought to Jesus all the sick and demon-possessed.*

ARE YOU excited when you hear about Jesus? The people of Bethsaida, Capernaum, and Korazin were stirred up. And why wouldn't they be?

News about Jesus was spreading: "We saw the Holy Spirit come on him." "We hear God's voice say, 'He's my son!'" "He's the Lamb of God!" "Did you see? He drives out demons." "Look at Peter's mom—she's well!"

The Good News of God's Kingdom come is coursing through the countryside, invading the hearts and minds of people eagerly searching for the Christ. They see evidence, "The Christ has come!" They're excited, and why wouldn't they be?

How about you? Where have you seen Jesus? Are you telling others how he has come to you? Are you eager to get up in the morning and read God's Word? Are you excited to sit down and pray, to be in conversation with the King?

Are you excited to know he is *your Savior!* Why wouldn't you be?

Pause and consider your passion level for Jesus – 1? (low) 10? (high) In between? Where do you want it? Where does Jesus want it?

A Good Place to Be

Purposeful Prayer

> Mark 1:35-38 *Very early in the morning, while it was still dark, Jesus got up, left the house and went off to a solitary place, where he prayed. 36 Simon and his companions went to look for him, 37 and when they found him, they exclaimed: "Everyone is looking for you!" 38 Jesus replied, "Let us go somewhere else — to the nearby villages — so I can preach there also. That is why I have come."*

WHAT DO you think about prayer? What's your response when someone tells you, "I'm praying for you." or "You need to pray about it."

One of the fascinating pictures of Jesus is how he gets up early in the morning and goes to be alone in prayer. Isn't it of interest to you that the Son of God purposefully goes to pray alone to the Father? Let that sink in.

Jesus needs the "alone time" with the Father before he begins his day. He needs to prepare for the ministry he's about to do. That ministry focus is his preaching as he says, *"This is why I have come."*

It is clear then, that one purpose of Jesus' prayers was to prepare for the preaching—the purpose for which he had come.

Now consider your own life. What is your purpose in life right now? Being a mom? A dad? Being a good worker? Being a student? Being a business leader? Being a child of God? Becoming someone with special purpose? Modeling the Son of God, what's a good thing to do in the purpose of your life?

Of course, it is to pray for God's strength, guidance, wisdom and peace in your purpose. That is what Jesus models for you. That is the Father's desire for you.

Pause and consider that as you pray into your life's purpose, your life will become more purposeful in Christ Jesus.

Be Clean

> Mark 1:40-42 *A man with leprosy came to him and begged him on his knees, "If you are willing, you can make me clean." 41 Filled with compassion, Jesus reached out his hand and touched the man. "I am willing," he said. "Be clean!" 42 Immediately the leprosy left him and he was cured.*

WOULD YOU stop for a moment and consider this: You are living life, doing all the usual things—working, going to school, playing sports, loving your friends, enjoying your children, being close to your spouse. Life has its challenges, and you're stressed out some days. But overall, life is good.

Then one day there's a mark on your skin. Your hands hurt. They bleed easily. You went to the priest. He told you, "You have leprosy."—a sentence to a living hell. You had to leave your loved ones, stay away from every one—no *physical touch,* unless the other person had leprosy, too. You could only see your family from a long distance. And you would never, ever touch them again, as you died inch by inch. Think of the horror.

Then one day the rabbi comes. You've heard the stories of his healing. Are they true? Dare you ask him? *"If you are willing, you can make me clean! You can heal me. I'll be able to touch my wife and children again. I can live again!"*

In his mercy, the rabbi say, *"Be clean!"* Oh, how unbelievable the joy! You are saved from leprosy's bondage!

Now consider how deadly sin separates families. Sin drives fathers and children and wives from their homes, never to touch their loved ones again. Do you long to go home?

Have you heard of Jesus? Dare you ask Jesus, "If you are willing, make me clean!"

Pause and consider how willing Jesus is to cleanse your sin.

A Good Place to Be

Remember Who Does It

> Mark 1:43-50 *Jesus sent him away at once with a strong warning:* 44 *"See that you don't tell this to anyone. But go, show yourself to the priest and offer the sacrifices that Moses commanded for your cleansing, as a testimony to them."* 45 *Instead he went out and began to talk freely, spreading the news. As a result, Jesus could no longer enter a town openly but stayed outside in lonely places. Yet the people still came to him from everywhere.*

WHEN YOU consider all the glorious healings the Gospels record, isn't it easy to say, "Jesus did it!" Would it not have been easy for him to say, "I did it!"

Instead, Jesus points the healed to the Father. Here he tells the now-clean man to go to the priests. God, the Father, had established laws by which a person would be declared clean to re-enter society. Jesus commanded the man to go and do what God had written in the Law of Moses.

When the healed man disobeyed and excitedly told his great news, he pointed the people too much to Jesus and too little to the Father. It caused a disruption in Jesus' ministry. He had to stay in lonely places, and he stopped his preaching for a time.

When you minister the Gospel and see God work—always give the praise to God. When you are healed in some way—physically, emotionally, spiritually, economically—never *praise* a person who has helped you. Instead, thank the godly person who has helped you and *praise the Father*. Your healing has come, as all things do, in the will of God through the power of the Spirit of God.

Pause and consider how God shows up in your life. Praise him!

The Word Preaches

> Mark 2:1-2 *A few days later, when Jesus again entered Capernaum, the people heard that he had come home. 2 So many gathered that there was no room left, not even outside the door, and he preached the word to them.*

CAN YOU imagine hearing the Word of God from the Word incarnate? (John 1:1) *In the beginning was the Word, and the Word was with God, and the Word was God.*

What caused the synagogue to fill to overflowing? Of course, it was the Word of God overflowing from heaven to earth. The glory of the Lord came down. People came because they knew the truth was in this place. Hungry for the truth, they came to hear the truth, to stand in the presence of God. The Word of the Lord is the glory of the Lord—his wonder and power and majesty—present among his people.

Here is Jesus, preaching the Word! No glitzy marketing efforts, no meal offered beforehand to attract newcomers.

Nope—preach the Word. Want to make a difference in someone's life? Preach the Word. Want help people walk with God? Preach the Word. Want to love your family more deeply? Preach the Word. Want to care for people at work? Preach the Word.

No, I don't mean you have to stand up and give a sermon, I mean you should speak to people about God. Share the truth of his love. Live the truth of his love. Clearly speak of how *"God so loved the world."* (John 3:16). Then live a life that demonstrates that love.

Begin your life each day in the Word of God then go and "preach" the Word.

Pause and consider the Word of God is most attractive when you speak it truthfully and live it lovingly.

A Good Place to Be

Now!

> Mark 2:3-5 Some men came, bringing to him a paralytic, carried by four of them. 4 Since they could not get him to Jesus because of the crowd, they made an opening in the roof above Jesus and, after digging through it, lowered the mat the paralyzed man was lying on.

ARE YOU a passionate person? If you're looking for a definition of passion, the men in this story certainly fit "passion". I always marvel at the paralyzed man's passion to see Jesus and his friends' passion to help him. How easy would it have been for them to walk away and say, "Later". I wonder if the man would have been healed if he said, "Later."

What about you? Do you passionately pursue Jesus, or do you say, "Later—not today. I don't feel like it. I'll get to it when it is more convenient for me."

Do you know what? You *won't* get to it later because you always have an excuse. You have things to do. You listen to distractions. You prefer mindless TV or meaningless conversations because your passion is "later" and not "now". You know what to do, but you make excuses because you like complaining about what you don't have instead of passionately pursuing what will change your life. Your soul is paralyzed with, "Later". The truth of "Later" is that it never comes until you say, "Now".

How about other areas of your life? Want a better job? Better marriage? Better friendships? Then stop living a paralyzed life. Get up and go where you need to be.

Pause and consider you need to start now.

Find Jesus Follow Jesus

Do You See?

> Mark 2:6-8 *Now some teachers of the law were sitting there, thinking to themselves, 7 "Why does this fellow talk like that? He's blaspheming! Who can forgive sins but God alone?" 8 Immediately Jesus knew in his spirit that this was what they were thinking in their hearts, and he said to them, "Why are you thinking these things?"*

HAVE YOU ever had the obvious walk right by you, and you didn't notice? Yesterday I was looking for some cd's for my sick computer. I searched many places and didn't find them. Today I was thinking about something else and saw this cd case in front of me, about 2 feet from where I was looking yesterday. In the case were the cd's I was seeking.

For centuries the Jews had looked for the prophesied Christ. Now he walks into this house, heals a paralyzed man and forgives the man's sins. Then the teachers look critically on Jesus and ask, "Who can forgive sins but God alone?"

Great question. Do you have a good answer? Indeed, my friends, only God *can* forgive sins. Let me see…if only God can forgive sins and Jesus forgives sins…hmm. Two plus two equals—don't tell me, I'll get it…someday.

How about you? Does God show up at your house to offer you his healing and forgiveness? Before you answer, let me ask this: Do you notice the people who offer you help? Did you receive a word of encouragement this week? Did your friend call you and "just listen"? Did someone invite you out for coffee? Did someone pray for you?

Do you think maybe God is showing up?

Pause and consider the obvious—Jesus might be right beside you.

A Good Place to Be

Jesus Shows You

> *Mark 2:10-12 But that you may know that the Son of Man has authority on earth to forgive sins . . . ." He said to the paralytic, 11 "I tell you, get up, take your mat and go home." 12 He got up, took his mat and walked out in full view of them all. This amazed everyone and they praised God, saying, "We have never seen anything like this!"*

DO YOU see how excited the people were? Jesus had healed the man. He stood up and walked. You can hear the excitement in the room, *"We have never seen anything like this!"*

Indeed, they had not seen what the personal God could personally do for them. They had heard of his marvelous deeds and might acts through of creation, freedom from Egypt, manna in the desert, and stunning victories over giants, but they had not seen God so remarkably in their midst.

Jesus was intent in his ministry to show his people and the world the God of the world. He clearly spoke the truth. He calmed the storms. He raised the dead. He healed the sick. He forgave sins.

Do you ask many questions about God's reality, his love, his presence in your life? Then look to Jesus. Look to see his life. Read the words. Hear the people's response. See his love amid the conflict. See his truth amid the doubt. See his life over death.

Jesus gave you a clear picture of the Living God. Are you eager to see him?

Pause and consider you only see a picture when you look at it.

Find Jesus Follow Jesus

Are You Uncomfortable?

> Mark 2:15-16 *While Jesus was having dinner at Levi's house, many tax collectors and "sinners" were eating with him and his disciples, for there were many who followed him. 16 When the teachers of the law who were Pharisees saw him eating with the "sinners" and tax collectors, they asked his disciples: "Why does he eat with tax collectors and 'sinners'?"*

DO YOU like to be comfortable? Then ministry probably isn't for you.

Consider Jesus' life. (You can read about it in the rest of "Mark" and the other Gospels.) Did he ever do anything in his ministry that made him comfortable? He went to the people who were sick, put himself in positions to be often criticized, attacked verbally and threatened physically. He went to the homes of such people as Levi, whom all the people hated because he was a tax collector. He even went to a stinking tomb to raise a dead man.

No, Jesus didn't seek comfort and neither should you if you desire to "minister" the Gospel. Ministry may require you to teach children who don't know the rules. Or you might need to spend time with teens who have no respect for you or anything, anyone else. Maybe it's uncomfortable to talk to people at work about Jesus. Possibly you need to go to a Third World country to minister to the hungry and desperate.

Do you feel God urging you to do something that makes you uncomfortable? To say to Jesus, "I'm not comfortable. Get someone else." negates the life of your Lord here on earth. Before you say, "No." pray for the Holy Spirit to give you strength and passion for your Lord. Then go. He has modeled for you what he expects of you. How will you respond?

Pause and consider Jesus' deadly discomfort of the cross is for you.

A Good Place to Be

Feast Forever

> *Mark 2:18-20 Now John's disciples and the Pharisees were fasting. Some people came and asked Jesus, "How is it that John's disciples and the disciples of the Pharisees are fasting, but yours are not?" 19 Jesus answered, "How can the guests of the bridegroom fast while he is with them? They cannot, so long as they have him with them. 20 But the time will come when the bridegroom will be taken from them, and on that day they will fast."*

IF YOU were invited to a wedding in Jesus' day, you were invited into a lengthy celebration. The bridegroom's arrival started the feast, and it was rude to not participate as a guest of the bridegroom. You "could not" fast during a feast!

Jesus' point here is that his disciples need to "feast" on him as much as possible while he is with them. He is preparing them to change the world with the truth of Jesus Christ. They will need *all* of Jesus' teaching to do what he will command them to do.

On the night before his crucifixion, Jesus reminded his disciples to "*take eat, this is my body broken for you*" (1 Corinthians 11:25) because he wanted them to know that he is fully a part of them. He has filled them with the bread of his truth, and his truth will energize them to the passion and power of the kingdom work ahead.

Jesus' disciples feasted on his teaching. You can, too. Spend time in the Bible and be filled with the nourishment of the truth of Jesus. This truth is what will strengthen you and nourish you to live each day in the fullness of the feast of life God desires for you.

Pause and consider the bridegroom has invited you to feast with him forever. Is there any reason you will not accept his invitation?

Room for the New

> Mark 2:21-22 *"No one sews a patch of unshrunk cloth on an old garment. If he does, the new piece will pull away from the old, making the tear worse. 22 And no one pours new wine into old wineskins. If he does, the wine will burst the skins, and both the wine and the wineskins will be ruined. No, he pours new wine into new wineskins."*

YOU'VE nursed the car along for years, spent too much money to keep it running. With all the time, effort and money, the car is still old and runs poorly.

Your life can be that way, can't it—not running well. It seems that regardless of what you try, nothing changes. You even went to a Bible study thinking, "Now everything will be fixed." But nothing changed. The same broken issues are still breaking your life. What to do?

What Jesus is teaching you here is that you can't keep putting new things into a heart and mind that is unable to receive them. New teachings, Jesus' teachings, will only "repair" the issues of your life if you have a heart desire to receive his teaching.

Oftentimes, as you read the Bible or hear it taught, you may say, "I'll check it out". You try it for a bit, but you're heart is still saying, "Maybe there's something else."

The Apostle Paul says (2 Cor 5:17) *Therefore, if anyone is in Christ, he is a new creation.* For Jesus' teachings to repair your life, you must become new in Jesus. That means you say, "Your will be done, Lord." You desire repair. And you pray earnestly for the Spirit of God to prepare your heart to be repaired in Christ.

Jesus came to make you new. Receive his teachings. Know the freedom of being new in him.

Pause and consider: Isn't it good the old car is gone, and you are no longer slave to the broken car?

A Good Place to Be

Who Do You Worship?

> Mark 2:27-28 Then he said to them, "The Sabbath was made for man, not man for the Sabbath. 28 So the Son of Man is Lord even of the Sabbath."

DO YOU think, perhaps, the church is about too many rules? Don't sing too loud. Don't dress that way. Don't lift your hands in praise. You better lift your hands in worship—or else. Yes, man-made rules can really restrict your view of God, can't they?

That was true during Jesus' day, too. God had given to Moses a law to "keep" the Sabbath as a day of rest, but he didn't give a long list of "do nots". However, the Jewish "church leaders" made sure they filled in the "blanks". They created numerous laws restricting activity on the Sabbath to the point they sharply criticized Jesus for healing and his disciples for eating!

As a result the Sabbath became a *thing to worship*. It was as if mankind had been created to obey rules on the Sabbath.

Jesus would have none of that. The Jewish traditions were stifling the Jews' opportunity to see the grace of God in the Sabbath rest. So he healed, and he allowed his disciples to pick some grain to eat (which the law permitted to feed weary travelers along the way).

Jesus wanted to bring the Sabbath back to its purpose—created for mankind to rest, not for mankind to be persecuted and worried about the oppressive rules.

What's happening in your church? The church was created for mankind to receive God's salvation through His Word. Is your church a place that causes you to wonder, "Am I doing everything right?" or is it a place to receive the freedom of God's grace and salvation?

Pause and consider God's Word to determine what is correct.

Find Jesus Follow Jesus

Who Killed the Gospel?

> Mark 3:1-6 *Another time he went into the synagogue, and a man with a shriveled hand was there. 2 Some of them were looking for a reason to accuse Jesus, so they watched him closely to see if he would heal him on the Sabbath. 3 Jesus said to the man with the shriveled hand, "Stand up in front of everyone." 4 Then Jesus asked them, "Which is lawful on the Sabbath: to do good or to do evil, to save life or to kill?" But they remained silent. 5 He looked around at them in anger and, deeply distressed at their stubborn hearts, said to the man, "Stretch out your hand." He stretched it out, and his hand was completely restored. 6 Then the Pharisees went out and began to plot with the Herodians how they might kill Jesus.*

DO YOU think this episode makes any sense? Jesus healed a man with a withered hand. Then the Pharisees looked for ways to kill him. Seriously? "Wake up, Pharisees! The Lord of Life is healing people. Celebrate him."

Before you get too critical, though, what about this? I've heard of people being offended because a church group worked on a Sunday to help some people in need. "It's the Sabbath. You don't *do those things* on a Sunday!"

Why not? Do you see the God, who came from the throne of heaven to minister into impoverished, disease-ridden communities? Do you see the God, who healed on the Sabbath and was *angry and deeply distressed over the stubborn, traditional hearts* around him? Would Jesus want you to heal people's needs on the Sabbath?

What do you think? When did holding back God become a mission of the church? The Pharisees killed Jesus. When did the church kill the gospel?

Pause and consider how Jesus loved this man. Go and do likewise.

A Good Place to Be

Does He Want You?

> Mark 3:13-15 *Jesus went up on a mountainside and called to him those he wanted, and they came to him. 14 He appointed twelve — designating them apostles — that they might be with him and that he might send them out to preach 15 and to have authority to drive out demons.*

DOES JESUS want you? Your first response may be, "I don't know. Should he?" or you might think, "I doubt it. I'm not good enough." Possibly you will think, "I sure hope so." What he desires you to think is, "Yes, he sure does!"

I hope and pray you know how much Jesus loves you, and that he does want you as his own. This scripture shows he called 12 men "he wanted" to be apostles. Do you see his vision for them? They would *"be with him and that he might send them out to preach"*. He wanted them because he wants you. Here's how I know.

Why would they be with him? Of course, it was to learn the truth of Jesus, the Savior the world. Once they learned that, they would go to preach. And what did they preach? Of course, it was the Gospel of salvation, the truth of Jesus, the Savior of the world.

And in the preaching they had authority to drive out demons. Why? Of course, it was to demonstrate the power of Jesus, the Savior of the world.

Now, why did he want these 12 men? It is because he wants you. Yes, here you see God's plan taking a dramatic step forward to teach, preach and show the truth of Jesus to the world. And now you are in the world. Yes, Jesus wanted these men because he wants you.

Pause and consider what else? Do *you* want Jesus?

Find Jesus Follow Jesus

Twelve Real Guys

> Mark 3:16-19 *These are the twelve he appointed: Simon (to whom he gave the name Peter); 17 James son of Zebedee and his brother John (to them he gave the name Boanerges, which means Sons of Thunder); 18 Andrew, Philip, Bartholomew, Matthew, Thomas, James son of Alphaeus, Thaddaeus, Simon the Zealot 19 and Judas Iscariot, who betrayed him.*

QUITE a draft day, isn't it? The Lord Jesus is the General Manager, the owner, the head coach wrapped into one. He has "drafted" 12 young men (most around the age of a college sports draftee) of various skills and abilities to form a world-changing team.

They are ordinary men with no particular reputation. He drafts them from the fishing boats, from the streets, from a tax collector's booth, from obscurity, and he calls them into an eternal purpose.

As a draftee comes into a professional team to learn a new system of how the team functions, these men will need training. They need to know who the opponent is. They need to know the plan to defeat the opponent. Jesus is calling these men to be on the team, and he needs their full commitment to be an effective team member. He calls them disciples.

Of course, the one nagging question is, "Why did Jesus choose Judas Iscariot, who betrayed him?" It seems to make no sense. But, in God's plan to send Jesus to the cross, there would have to be one close to Jesus who would reject and betray him. It seems so unfair that Jesus would purposefully call one to betray him.

The reality is, though, the ultimate unfairness in our lives is that God so loved you, a sinner, that Jesus, the only one without sin, would die for you. Makes no sense—we get what we don't deserve.

Pause and consider that even though our hearts betray Jesus, he has chosen you to be his.

A Good Place to Be

Family First?

> Mark 3:20-21 Then Jesus entered a house, and again a crowd gathered, so that he and his disciples were not even able to eat. 21 When his family heard about this, they went to take charge of him, for they said, "He is out of his mind."
>
> Mark 3:33 "Who are my mother and my brothers?" he asked.

YOU likely put a high priority on family life. You desire to nurture and care for them. God desires you do so.

Jesus' family went out to get him. He was so intense in his work, he hadn't eaten. They likely feared for him, also, because of the large crowds around him. They thought it best to go get Jesus and bring him home.

That was good of them from a human point of view, but it was not what God wanted them to do. It's not what Jesus needed to do right then. He was about his work. There's family time and there's "mission of God" time. Jesus' passion was to be on mission to proclaim the Word of God through his teaching and healing. This was his highest priority.

Yes, Jesus may have been hungry, but he knew he'd survive – remember 40 days in the desert? Yes, people were opposing him, but he certainly would defend himself – remember 40 days against the devil?

When Jesus rhetorically asks, "Who are my mother and my brothers?" He's saying, "My mission is my purpose. My work is to save all my people. I cannot be distracted, and I must do it."

Pause and consider Jesus did not turn from his mission to take you home.

Find Jesus Follow Jesus

Untie the Gospel

> Mark 3:22-27 And the teachers of the law who came down from Jerusalem said, "He is possessed by Beelzebub! By the prince of demons he is driving out demons." 23 So Jesus called them and spoke to them in parables: "How can Satan drive out Satan? 24 If a kingdom is divided against itself, that kingdom cannot stand. 25 If a house is divided against itself, that house cannot stand. 26 And if Satan opposes himself and is divided, he cannot stand; his end has come. 27 In fact, no one can enter a strong man's house and carry off his possessions unless he first ties up the strong man. Then he can rob his house.

LOOKING for a way to discredit the demon-driving-out miracles Jesus is doing, the teachers of the law claim he is Satan. After all, Satan is the only one who could cause the demons to go away.

Jesus' reply is essentially, "That's ridiculous. A house is divided against cannot stand."

Let's shift the view and look at the church and ask, "What, too often, holds back the purpose of the church?" There are many influences that can stop a church "dead" in its mission. Unfortunately one of those mission-killing factors is how we "tie up" Jesus, the "strong man".

Think how God's house is too often divided against itself with, "I want things my way?" or "I'm too busy to help." or "We never did it that way before." Ministries are left undone because we "tie up" the God we claim to worship with, "Later." and "Not me." God cannot work on hearts tied to their own preferences. He needs hearts untied for him.

Pause and consider your heart. Is it bound by "me", or in Jesus is it free?

A Good Place to Be

Trust the Spirit

> *Mark 3:22 And the teachers of the law who came down from Jerusalem said, "He is possessed by Beelzebub! By the prince of demons he is driving out demons."*
> &
> *Mark 3:28-29 "I tell you the truth, all the sins and blasphemies of men will be forgiven them. But whoever blasphemes against the Holy Spirit will never be forgiven; he is guilty of an eternal sin."*

YOU SAY, "I thought God forgave all sins. What's this eternal sin?"

This does seem to contradict the picture of the all-forgiving God who offers you forgiveness and salvation if (Romans 10:9) *you confess with your mouth, "Jesus is Lord," and believe in your heart that God raised him from the dead, you will be saved.*

How can there be any eternal sin?

When you look at Mark 3:22, you see the teachers refusing to believe the Holy Spirit is working to drive demons from people. They are giving the credit due God to Satan.

Now is it clear why this is an eternal, unforgiveable sin? These men refuse to give praise and worship to the holy God, who clearly shows his power to heal.

Do you get that way? Do you refuse, first of all, to believe the Holy Spirit can and will do miracles in your life? Do you believe the Holy Spirit has the power to heal your disease, to guide your life, and to save you from Hell?

Or, do you give credit of the good things in your life to luck, coincidence and chance? If so, you are neglecting the power of the Holy Spirit. You must stop that false thinking and turn to trust the truth of the Spirit in your life.

Believe in the Spirit. He is alive and powerful. He loves you.

Pause and consider: How is anything possible without the living Spirit of God?

Find Jesus Follow Jesus

Got Life?

> Mark 4: 3-8 "Listen! A farmer went out to sow his seed. 4 As he was scattering the seed, some fell along the path, and the birds came and ate it up. 5 Some fell on rocky places, where it did not have much soil. It sprang up quickly, because the soil was shallow. 6 But when the sun came up, the plants were scorched, and they withered because they had no root. 7 Other seed fell among thorns, which grew up and choked the plants, so that they did not bear grain. 8 Still other seed fell on good soil. It came up, grew and produced a crop, multiplying thirty, sixty, or even a hundred times."

DO YOU desire to be good soil? Think of how life-giving is this picture that Jesus draws for you.

What a joy it is to travel America and see bountiful crops of many types fill the fields. America's rich soil and ample water is one reason for our wealth.

Jesus wants you to be wealthy in his truth. As good soil needs living organisms to grow healthy crops, you must have the living word of God in you. God's living word grows living truth. Living truth grows you strong against temptation and causes you to produce good fruit in your marriage, your children and your relationships.

I don't know anyone who has had a garden and purposely ignored it, causing it to become arid, dry and lifeless. But I know many, many people who have an arid, lifeless faith because they do not seek the life-growing power of God's Word for their lives.

I don't understand why it is so difficult to get people to read the Bible. Do you?

Pause and consider that Life comes from Life. What is your life source?

A Good Place to Be

Sing the Light

> *Mark 4:21-23 He said to them, "Do you bring in a lamp to put it under a bowl or a bed? Instead, don't you put it on its stand? 22 For whatever is hidden is meant to be disclosed, and whatever is concealed is meant to be brought out into the open. 23 If anyone has ears to hear, let him hear."*

THREE years ago on the show "Britian's Got Talent", Susan Boyle, a very ordinary-looking woman, stunned everyone with her extraordinary, emotional rendition of "I Dreamed a Dream".

Susan's dream was to sing as Elaine Paige, one of Britain's top show tune singers. Before she sang, all laughed at the silly woman with a silly dream. They stood and shouted approval after Susan's song.

That night, Susan Boyle's light burst forth onto the world's stage. Millions of ears heard. To date, this performance on YouTube has 13,640,293 hits. (Elaine Paige's YouTube songs aren't even close.)

The people of the world crave the triumph of dreams. They crave the suppressed light bursting forth.

2,000 years ago, Jesus burst forth with the irrepressible Light of God's truth onto the world stage. When you claim Jesus as your Lord and Savior, that Light is in you and for you.

And so I ask, "What will you do with the Light?" Do you suppress the Light because you don't trust Jesus' truth? Are you ridiculed because others think the Light is silly? Do you know you have it, but you are afraid to "sing it"?

I want to tell you something. Never mind the doubters. The world craves Jesus' Light. Give it to them. Stand up and sing it out. It is Jesus' song in you. Let those who have ears, hear Jesus' truth from you.

Pause and consider, if Susan Boyle kept quiet, no one would know.

Hear It. Use It.

> Mark 4:24-25 *"Consider carefully what you hear,"* he continued. *"With the measure you use, it will be measured to you — and even more. 25 Whoever has will be given more; whoever does not have, even what he has will be taken from him."*

DO YOU see the ways this scripture is true for you?

If you're a student who needs to pass a class, you pay attention to enough information to get you through. If you're a student who really wants to be good at something, you pay really close attention to know as much as you can know.

If for example, you want to be a great carpenter, the more you know and the more you put what you know to use, the greater you will be "measured" by those for whom you build.

One of my big questions in ministry is this: Why don't people want to know as much of God as possible?

My second big question is: Why don't people want to use God's truth in their daily lives?

Jesus says it is critical first that you hear God's truth (that can be through reading, listening to sermons, etc.) to learn the truth. Then it is *mandatory* to put God's truth into action. If you don't, you will lose it.

If you're a carpenter, pianist, teacher, accountant, salesperson, etc., and you fail to use what you know, you will lose what you know.

The same is true of God's truth. If you hear it, then put it away, you will lose it. And God will judge you for your lack of faith.

The glorious promise here, though, is that when you begin to use God's truth it will grow to be a blessing to you and to all around you.

Pause and consider that anything you don't use is useless.

| A Good Place to Be

Ready for the Harvest?

> Mark 4:26-29 He also said, "This is what the kingdom of God is like. A man scatters seed on the ground. 27 Night and day, whether he sleeps or gets up, the seed sprouts and grows, though he does not know how. 28 All by itself the soil produces grain — first the stalk, then the head, then the full kernel in the head. 29 As soon as the grain is ripe, he puts the sickle to it, because the harvest has come."

YOU might be wondering, "Ready for what harvest?" I hope you're wondering this. The answer is crucial to your eternal future.

Jesus gives a very clear Kingdom truth here. He is the farmer who plants the seed, the Truth of Jesus Christ. Once the truth is planted into good soil, it will not stop. It will root and prosper.

As sun and rain nurture a plant to grow, the Truth of Jesus nurtures you to grow and mature in the truth.

What happens when the plant has a full kernel? The kernel becomes food for some and new seed for new plants. What happens when you mature in Jesus' truth? You produce seed.

You become "food" to feed people hungry for the truth, and you become seed to plant new truth into new soil. You tell your friends. You tell your children. The Kingdom of God grows through you.

Then what? As with any plant, your life here will end. One day God will "harvest" your life from earth into eternal life. The thing is, you don't know when that will be. Thus, I return to my question, "Ready for the harvest?"

What do you say? Is Jesus' truth planted, growing and maturing in you?

Pause and consider carefully your answer. Romans 10:9 offers you the way to say, "Yes, I am ready for the harvest."

Kingdom Growing Power

> Mark 4:30-32 Again he said, "What shall we say the kingdom of God is like, or what parable shall we use to describe it? 31 It is like a mustard seed, which is the smallest seed you plant in the ground. 32 Yet when planted, it grows and becomes the largest of all garden plants, with such big branches that the birds of the air can perch in its shade."

HAVE you ever been around a mustard plant? They're not so big. As a boy on the farm I would walk the grain and hay fields to pull up mustard plants and put them in a bag. It was the only way 50 years ago to remove the weed and save the crop.

So what's Jesus talking about here—a mustard seed growing into a huge plant with branches for birds to sit on?

He is talking about Kingdom growing. The Kingdom of God is supernatural. God created the heavens and the earth and set a natural order to the universe. Then sin broke into his creation. As a consequence, God's creation, especially mankind, groans under sin's weight. Now God has stepped in to transform the natural sin with his supernatural power.

In the power of God, Jesus supernaturally transforms blindness to sight, lameness to strength, leprosy to wholeness, death to life, and sin to salvation.

When you accept Jesus' salvation, you have at your disposal that same supernatural power through the Holy Spirit. The Spirit grows your heart to love, to forgive, to seek God, to worship God, to trust his mercy, to know his grace, and to know new life in his risen life. Yes, whatever you face, the Spirit's supernatural power is available to supernaturally strengthen and shelter you.

Pause and consider how you can be transformed in God's power.

A Good Place to Be

Learn It

> Mark 4:33-34 With many similar parables Jesus spoke the word to them, as much as they could understand. 34 He did not say anything to them without using a parable. But when he was alone with his own disciples, he explained everything.

DO YOU want to get to know Jesus really well? Then become a disciple. What does a disciple do? He or she spends a good amount of time with Jesus.

Many times in the accounts of Jesus' ministry, you'll see him enter into teaching time with only his disciples. The disciples want to know all Jesus knows and do what Jesus does to become like their rabbi. When they follow Jesus, they literally follow him as closely as they can. They crowd around him as he walks. They sit or stand close to him as he teaches. They are attentive. They ask questions. Their disciplined following causes Jesus' ways to become their ways.

How do you become a disciple? You can literally sit with his Word. You can also sit with others to ask questions and learn his word. You can listen to preaching in church and teachings on TV and on the radio. Podcasts and websites are available with some of the world's best teachers free of charge. God's Word is everywhere. You just have to sit down and hear it.

You might say, "That's too much." And I will say, "How could you get too much of the eternal God? How could you get too much of the God who freely offers you eternal life?"

Why is he last on your list? Why are you always saying, "Not now." when you are invited to a Bible study?

When will you learn if not now?

Pause and consider: each day you wait, you miss knowing Jesus.

Find Jesus Follow Jesus

Jesus' Calm

Mark 4:35-40 That day when evening came, he said to his disciples, "Let us go over to the other side." 36 Leaving the crowd behind, they took him along, just as he was, in the boat. There were also other boats with him. 37 A furious squall came up, and the waves broke over the boat, so that it was nearly swamped. 38 Jesus was in the stern, sleeping on a cushion. The disciples woke him and said to him, "Teacher, don't you care if we drown?" 39 He got up, rebuked the wind and said to the waves, "Quiet! Be still!" Then the wind died down and it was completely calm. 40 He said to his disciples, "Why are you so afraid? Do you still have no faith?"

WHAT DO you think? Does Jesus care if you drown? When life's storms wash over you and the winds of doubt, worry and pain blow against you, don't you want to know, "Jesus, don't you care if I drown?"

Jesus clearly shows here that he does care. He does have the power to save you from the storms. And he will use it.

It's too easy, isn't it, to focus on the storms even though the Savior is with you? The disciples could have called on Jesus when the clouds were forming and the wind increasing, but they focused on dealing with the storms in their own way. After all, some were experienced on the sea and knew how to handle a boat. They could "do it themselves".

But the storm got too big for them. Their fear got too big for them. Desperately they turned to Jesus. And Jesus came to quiet the storm with his words.

What storms rage around you? You can't handle them yourself. Jesus can. Have that faith in his power to calm the storm.

Pause and consider how Jesus speaks calm.

A Good Place to Be

Worship Him

> Mark 4:41 They were terrified and asked each other, "Who is this? Even the wind and the waves obey him!"

THE DISCIPLES had been with Jesus for some time when he calmed the storm on the sea. Perhaps this is the first time they feared him.

What caused their fear? They see the power of Jesus' words. They see Jesus' Lordship over nature. They see Jesus' holiness in that power.

When they realize they could be in the presence of (Psalms 146:6) *the Maker of heaven and earth, the sea, and everything in them* — what could they do but tremble in fear.

His unlimited power stood next to their faithless lives. His sovereign authority determined the destiny of their sin-filled souls. His all-knowing mind dwarfed their limited understanding. He held their souls in his hand. Why would they not tremble in fear?

Yes, now they are beginning to more clearly see who this Jesus is. They are growing in their understanding that their rabbi is the Lord of Hosts. They have seen the power of his words, and they are afraid.

Their fear can cause them to run from their Lord, or their fear can cause them to turn their minds to a greater understanding of their Lord. They were on a boat. They had to stay, and they would learn more. As it says in Proverbs 9:10-11
"The fear of the Lord is the beginning of wisdom, and knowledge of the Holy One is understanding."

Now they begin to understand that they must *really* listen to their rabbi. They begin to understand his words will not only calm the winds, his words will even transform their lives.

Pause and consider that truly knowing Jesus will change your life. Fearful, isn't it?

Find Jesus Follow Jesus

Irresistible Jesus

> Mark 5:1-5 They went across the lake to the region of the Gerasenes. 2 When Jesus got out of the boat, a man with an evil spirit came from the tombs to meet him. 3 This man lived in the tombs, and no one could bind him any more, not even with a chain. 4 For he had often been chained hand and foot, but he tore the chains apart and broke the irons on his feet. No one was strong enough to subdue him. 5 Night and day among the tombs and in the hills he would cry out and cut himself with stones.

CAN YOU imagine anything so horrible? This man lived among the dead. He was insane. He was incredibly strong and opposed all who came near him. He cut himself with stones. He's certainly the kind of man you would avoid.

But wait a minute. What happened? He goes to see Jesus. You'll see in the next 2 readings what Jesus does in response. But first, why does this deranged, demon-possessed man go to meet Jesus?

Do you think Jesus was irresistible? I think so. Why wouldn't he be? The Bible records numerous times that great crowds, (many people, large numbers, etc.) went to see him. He was as a "rabbi rock star"—God's Son, the Light of the world, the Holy One of God.

Jesus was the one who healed. He spoke and people were in awe. He called, then men dropped their nets and they followed.

The demons control this man; yet, Jesus is irresistible to even them. When the Lord shows up, they must go to him. These demons know he is their Master.

How about you? What do you know about Jesus? You know enough to know you must go to him. What's stopping you?

Pause and consider anew the steps you must take to Jesus.

A Good Place to Be

Subject to the King

> Mark 5:6-10 *When he saw Jesus from a distance, he ran and fell on his knees in front of him. 7 He shouted at the top of his voice, "What do you want with me, Jesus, Son of the Most High God? Swear to God that you won't torture me!" 8 For Jesus had said to him, "Come out of this man, you evil spirit!" 9 Then Jesus asked him, "What is your name?" "My name is Legion," he replied, "for we are many." 10 And he begged Jesus again and again not to send them out of the area.*

WHAT WOULD it be like if you lived in total subjection to a king? A "subject" of the king, you would be subjected to his commands. His authority would absolutely rule your life.

Scripture repeatedly shows the demons know Jesus is the one who will condemn them to eternal punishment as he (Revelation 19:15) *"will rule them with an iron scepter."* They know his power is ultimate. When the Christ acts, the Christ acts and nothing will hold him back.

How about you? Do you believe that? If Christ is your Savior, he is also your King. You are a citizen of the Kingdom of God. A subject of the King, you are subject to the King.

Do you receive his words as the authority of your life? Do you pray for mercy in the authority of his forgiveness of your sins? Do you pray for his kingly power to heal the broken relationships, the hurts in your life?

Pray to Jesus as the ultimate authority of your life because he is.

Pause and consider that one day you will stand before Jesus' authority. Will you beg for mercy or praise him for his mercy?

Find Jesus Follow Jesus

What Matters?

> Mark 5:11-15 *A large herd of pigs was feeding on the nearby hillside. 12 The demons begged Jesus, "Send us among the pigs; allow us to go into them." 13 He gave them permission, and the evil spirits came out and went into the pigs. The herd, about two thousand in number, rushed down the steep bank into the lake and were drowned. 14 Those tending the pigs ran off and reported this in the town and countryside, and the people went out to see what had happened. 15 When they came to Jesus, they saw the man who had been possessed by the legion of demons, sitting there, dressed and in his right mind; and they were afraid.*

WHAT DO you think? Is it better to restore one man's life—or save the swine?

Legion—the demons—pleads with Jesus, *"Send us among the pigs; allow us to go into them."* Why? They want to destroy the swine. They want to turn the people against Jesus as they accuse, "He killed the swine!"

What are Jesus' purposes here? One, he wants to save the man, to deliver him from evil. Two, he wants to test these Gentiles. What will they consider good? What will be their reaction to the One who delivers them from evil?

As you see, they were afraid. Jesus had saved a man, but the swine died. That's lost income for some. Even though Legion had mocked and harassed them through the man, they were more afraid they had lost their livelihood. They were afraid the One who had delivered them from evil could not give them that day their daily "bread" – a new way of life.

They preferred the swine over the salvation.

Pause and consider: what evil rules your life? Do you trust Jesus to deliver you? Do you want him to?

A Good Place to Be

How About Jesus!

> Mark 5:16-17 Those who had seen it told the people what had happened to the demon-possessed man — and told about the pigs as well. 17 Then the people began to plead with Jesus to leave their region.

DO YOU see how the Gentiles send Jesus away? He healed a man. He disturbed their traditions. He entered into their way of life and made changes. He brought salvation to the land, and they said, "Go."

Why would they do such a thing? Why would you do such a thing?

You say, "I'd never send Jesus away." Wouldn't you? Haven't you? How about that time you told a "little white lie" to avoid blame for a costly error? How about when you spent too much time at work and missed your child's school program? How about when you were angry with your spouse—and it was really your own fault? How about when you said, "Why pray? God doesn't care?" How about when you said, "I can't change. That's me, like it or not."

How about this? How about rejoicing that Jesus has come into your life? How about embracing his transforming power? How about thanking him for the ways he protects you? How about worshiping him as Lord? How about reading his Word and telling others? How about living a life, believing in his power to change you, to heal you, to care for you, and to love you?

Pause and consider: The people of the Gerasenes didn't want Jesus' changes? How about it?

Find Jesus Follow Jesus

Earnestly Approaching Jesus

> Mark 5:21-24 When Jesus had again crossed over by boat to the other side of the lake, a large crowd gathered around him while he was by the lake. 22 Then one of the synagogue rulers, named Jairus, came there. Seeing Jesus, he fell at his feet 23 and pleaded earnestly with him, "My little daughter is dying. Please come and put your hands on her so that she will be healed and live." 24 So Jesus went with him. A large crowd followed and pressed around him.

DO YOU see how the people and Jairus earnestly sought Jesus as he returned to Capernaum?

From the beginning of his Gospel, Mark has been telling the story of how people earnestly came to the Jordan to repent and be baptized to prepare to see the Savior. And when the Savior shows up, the news spreads. People are amazed. Huge crowds earnestly seek him. God's people are starving for the Bread of Life. They are parched for the Living Water. They are lost for lack of a Good Shepherd.

In Jesus they see the One who can fill their spiritual hunger, ease their hopeless thirst and guide their directionless lives. Yes, why wouldn't they earnestly seek him as did Jairus, who fell at Jesus' feet to plead with him? His daughter is dying. He earnestly needs the one who can heal!

How do you go to Jesus? Do you think, "I'll pray once and see if anything happens." "If I have time, I'll read some Bible today."

That's no way to go to the Savior. You need him, too, to fill you, quench your thirst and lead you to healing. He deserves your full attention.

Pause and consider how excited you are to see your best friend. Are you as excited to go to the Savior?

A Good Place to Be

Suffering Jesus

> *Mark 5:25-29 And a woman was there who had been subject to bleeding for twelve years. 26 She had suffered a great deal under the care of many doctors and had spent all she had, yet instead of getting better she grew worse. 27 When she heard about Jesus, she came up behind him in the crowd and touched his cloak, 28 because she thought, "If I just touch his clothes, I will be healed." 29 Immediately her bleeding stopped and she felt in her body that she was freed from her suffering.*

"**FREED** from her suffering"…an incredible statement isn't it? How you long for yourself or for someone you know to be freed from suffering. Suffering—a deep hurt physically that won't quit, a penetrating hurt psychologically that shows up with every thought. What do you do with the suffering?

It's easy for me to say, "Be like the bleeding woman. She went to Jesus, and he healed her." But what would have happened if he didn't heal her? Would you know her? No. You hear of the healed. What happens to the unhealed? Where's Jesus in their suffering? Where's Jesus in your suffering?

He's right there. Do you see him? He's at the whipping post. The Roman soldiers are lashing him to unbearable suffering for you.

Do you see him? The Roman executors are driving big spikes through his wrists. Now they are lifting his suffering body on a cross. Do you see him hanging there? Why is he experiencing that suffering pain? Of course, he suffers for you.

Yes, Jesus heals some now. Some he heals after "12 years". Some he does not heal in this life.

Yet, Jesus has suffered to heal you for eternity. Call on Jesus as Lord and be healed forever.

Pause and consider how you need to touch Jesus to know his healing power.

Find Jesus Follow Jesus

Real Power

> Mark 5:30-32 *At once Jesus realized that power had gone out from him. He turned around in the crowd and asked, "Who touched my clothes?" 31 "You see the people crowding against you, "his disciples answered, "and yet you can ask, 'Who touched me?'" 32 But Jesus kept looking around to see who had done it.*

YOU know Jesus' healing power is real here, don't you. His power is so much a part of him he *feels* it flow out of him.

The Gospels record one miraculous, power-filled scene after another. The events happen so quickly, you can easily miss them. Demons gone, the blind see, the deaf hear. The words of life are proclaimed, and lives are changed forever.

The wonder of Jesus power demonstration is that he didn't stop—ever. His power is still going into the world right now. This past week in our town, 75 teens came to faith in him at a rally at the high school. A junior high boy known for causing trouble has found new life. A teen turned from her suicide desires. A family found comfort in their deep sorrow. A 4-year-old boy came to church and is excited for Jesus. A young boy has found peace from his worries. A young mom has begun to see joy and hope in her life once again. A teen has been rescued from an abusive home.

"Where's Jesus?" You ask. He's right here in the crowd of hurt, hopelessness, pain, doubts, fears, disease and worry. Yes, Jesus walks right into these places. And when you touch him, his real, alive and life-changing power flows from him.

Do you want this in your life? Then go touch him. Grab onto him. Hold onto him. Let his power flow to you.

Pause and consider Jesus' power never is unplugged.

A Good Place to Be

Why Bother Jesus?

> *Mark 5:33-36 Then the woman, knowing what had happened to her, came and fell at his feet and, trembling with fear, told him the whole truth. 34 He said to her, "Daughter, your faith has healed you. Go in peace and be freed from your suffering." 35 While Jesus was still speaking, some men came from the house of Jairus, the synagogue ruler. "Your daughter is dead," they said. "Why bother the teacher further?" 36 Ignoring what they said, Jesus told the synagogue ruler, "Don't be afraid; just believe."*

HERE is a woman healed and then she is fearful she has stepped beyond her bounds. Here is a man seeking healing for his daughter. Then he hears the news she is dead. Then Jesus assures him, "Do not be afraid."

Fear pops up in so many places, doesn't it? "I'm afraid to go to Jesus. He might say I'm too guilty." Or "I'm afraid. I have no hope for my future." Or "I'm afraid to tell anyone how Jesus has healed me. They will laugh at me. They'll think I'm crazy."

Jesus tells you and shows you here that there is no room for fear in his Kingdom. He welcomes you to come to him. He offers you hope amid disease and even death because he conquers all things that oppose him. He offers to you his love as you seek him and go touch him.

When Jesus says, "Don't be afraid, just believe." he is offering himself to the woman, to Jairus, to the crowd around him, and to you.

Jesus wants you to know in the turmoil of fear and emotions from all directions, you can turn and focus on him.

Turn to Jesus. As each new emotion comes to you, say his name. Touch his cloak. Hear his love. Your fear will go.

Pause and consider Jesus' presence quiets your emotions.

Get Up and Live!

> Mark 5:37-42 *He did not let anyone follow him except Peter, James and John the brother of James. 38 When they came to the home of the synagogue ruler, Jesus saw a commotion, with people crying and wailing loudly. 39 He went in and said to them, "Why all this commotion and wailing? The child is not dead but asleep." 40 But they laughed at him. After he put them all out, he took the child's father and mother and the disciples who were with him, and went in where the child was. 41 He took her by the hand and said to her, "Talitha koum!" (which means, "Little girl, I say to you, get up!"). 42 Immediately the girl stood up and walked around (she was twelve years old). At this they were completely astonished.*

DO YOU ever wonder why Jesus "put them all out" of the house? Wouldn't it have been good for Jairus' friends and relatives to personally witness the little girl's resurrection?

Jesus is the Glory of the Lord come to earth to reveal the power of the Kingdom of God. He is prophecy fulfilled. (Isaiah 40:5) *"And the glory of the Lord will be revealed, and all mankind together will see it. For the mouth of the Lord has spoken."*

Yes, on that day, in this tiny home came the Glory of the Lord. He spoke to the mockers and said, "Be gone!" He spoke to Death and said, "Be gone!" The Glory of the Lord had come, and there is no room for the sin of unbelief. There is no room for death.

What about you? Do you mock the Glory of the Lord standing at your door? Or do you invite him in to exhibit the power of the Kingdom come?

Pause and consider the King of Glory wants to enter into your home.

A Good Place to Be

Why Not Tell?

> *Mark 5:43 He gave strict orders not to let anyone know about this, and told them to give her something to eat.*

JESUS has resurrected a young girl from her death bed. Call back the mourners. Call back the family waiting outside the house. Run to the streets and proclaim, "My daughter is alive! She was dead, but now she lives!"

But wait. The Lord of Life says, "Don't tell." You look at him and wonder, "Why not? This is awesome news, Jesus! I *have* to let people know."

Yes, why would Jesus issue this request for silence regarding the girl's resurrection? He says this to others he heals. Most ignore him and go tell anyway.

My thought here is that Jesus was trying to protect his ministry and his mission. We see before this that huge crowds were pressing around him. People were desperately seeking him for their physical healing. And as he obliged them, the pressing crowds grew larger. "Heal me now, Jesus!" they might have called.

Although his healing power was vital to his ministry, Jesus' main ministry was to preach the Gospel and to minister eternal healing, eternal life, to the world. It seems Jesus was concerned here that people would focus too much on the quick healing and focus too little on his eternal healing.

Jesus wasn't a miracle worker for his own sake. Jesus' primary mission was to proclaim the power of God had come for the eternal salvation of the world. He could not allow the pressing crowds, seeking a "quick fix" to their lives keep him from his mission.

Pause and consider: Are you after Jesus for a "quick fix" for your life or for eternal life?

Find Jesus Follow Jesus

He Had to Tell

> Mark 6:1-3 Jesus left there and went to his hometown, accompanied by his disciples. 2 When the Sabbath came, he began to teach in the synagogue, and many who heard him were amazed. "Where did this man get these things?" they asked. "What's this wisdom that has been given him that he even does miracles! 3 Isn't this the carpenter? Isn't this Mary's son and the brother of James, Joseph, Judas and Simon? Aren't his sisters here with us?" And they took offense at him.

SOMETHING from many years ago bothers me. It is something I said, and it is someone's attitude in response to my words.

I was working with a group of people, and someone was talking about a subject I happened to know something about. The person was well-intentioned and offered some good information, but the person also shared some misinformation. If it were intentional you would call them lies, but it wasn't intentional. It was information that many people thought was true, but I knew the facts. So, what would I do?

I tried to correct the misinformation. I had no intention to make the other person look bad, but what was said was totally wrong. I don't think my words were well received. Maybe I should have kept quiet. It wasn't a life or death matter.

But what if it were? What if the misinformation would lead someone to death—eternal death? Would I be obliged to speak up then? Of course I would. I would have to try my best to guide the person to the life-giving facts.

That's what Jesus did. He spoke into the misinformation. He corrected the lies. And his listeners hated him. They hated the truth. They hated his authority. They hated the way to life. Jesus couldn't keep still. He had the way to life, and the people needed to know.

Pause and consider your obligation to know the truth and to tell the truth. Your response is to the truth.

A Good Place to Be

Faith Response

> Mark 6:4-6 Jesus said to them, "Only in his hometown, among his relatives and in his own house is a prophet without honor." 5 He could not do any miracles there, except lay his hands on a few sick people and heal them. 6 And he was amazed at their lack of faith. Then Jesus went around teaching from village to village.

ARE YOU looking for God to do a power move in your life? Do you desire he bring change to you, your family or your church? What do you need to "do" to make that happen? A common answer might be, "Have faith."

That certainly seems to be what Jesus is saying here. He could do very few miracles because the people of his hometown area had little faith in him. Yet, there are times when he acts in great power—he calms the storms, he raises the dead, he distributes a few loaves and fish to thousands—when no one around him has faith he can do such things. What blocks his miraculous healings here?

What seems to be happening is the people's continuing doubt. They have heard of his miracles, he has done a few miracles, but their faith remains locked in their perception of Jesus as a "local" man. Once presented with the Gospel, they have repeatedly rejected it. They deny Jesus' authority as the Christ. As a result he will deny to them the power of the Christ.

How has Jesus presented himself to you? Have you heard his truth, yet questioned, even rejected the truth? Do you doubt Jesus is alive for you right now? Do you think, perhaps, you're not worthy of his miracles? Do you rely on worldly ways to guide your life?

Pause and consider the evidence of Jesus' authority to heal, to transform and to give life. Have faith in him.

Time to Act

> Mark 6:7 Calling the Twelve to him, he sent them out two by two and gave them authority over evil spirits.

HERE'S the first demonstration of Jesus transferring his power to his disciples. Jesus can keep doing his saving work among his people, but much more can be done as he empowers his disciples to go and to what he does.

This is one of the great lessons of the New Testament. Jesus came to administer the power of heaven on the earth. Then he empowered his disciples to do likewise. On the day of Pentecost, as the Spirit comes upon these same disciples (minus Judas), Jesus is transferring the heavenly power to earth until the day of his return.

Disciples are people disciplined to do the work of God on earth. They also are empowered to do the work of God on earth that his name be known.

This is the purpose of the church. A church is to be filled with Jesus' disciples who are empowered by the Spirit to do the work of God in the world. Disciples are to "go out" and offer Jesus to the world through helping, teaching, praying and healing. Is that something you and your church are doing?

When you assess your own life with Jesus, can you call yourself his disciple? Do you obey where he has called you to go? Do you understand what he wants you to do? Do you trust his authority on your life to do so?

Jesus gave 12 "newcomers" authority to teach and heal. Why wouldn't he do the same for you?

Pause and consider the authority of Jesus is for you, too.

| A Good Place to Be

Will You?

> Mark 6:8-10 *These were his instructions: "Take nothing for the journey except a staff — no bread, no bag, no money in your belts. 9 Wear sandals but not an extra tunic. 10 Whenever you enter a house, stay there until you leave that town.*

WHEN someone comes to me and asks, "How do I know God's will for my life?" I think they already know the answer. Their challenge is having the faith to follow Jesus into his will.

There's a distinct "survival mechanism" in your mind that tells you, "Be sure you have all you need before you go where God is calling you. Get your finances in line. Get your faith built up. Get your friends and church behind you. Be sure you know what you will do if things don't "work out". Be sure you're comfortable with going. Be sure you've thought of all the possibilities, covered all the bases. Be sure there are no surprises."

What do you think the Apostles thought when Jesus gave them these instructions? They had minimal supplies, only a walking stick. Their life support—food, water, shelter—would come from people they would meet along the way. They had absolutely no assurance of what would happen beyond the Savior's words.

And that's the thing, isn't it? What you really need to follow God into his will for your life is a trust in the Savior's words. His teachings to his disciples included powerful faith lessons to know God's will. One of those lessons was in the "going and doing".

If you seek God's will for your life, you must be willing to follow him with the bare essentials—your faith, hope and love in him—to go and do what he has called you to do. God's will never be clear to you in any other way.

Pause and consider how simple it is for God to give you what you need. After all, he gave you life.

Getting It Done

> Mark 6:11 *"And if any place will not welcome you or listen to you, shake the dust off your feet when you leave, as a testimony against them."*

A SAD reality is that not all will welcome Jesus. I see this nearly every day in some way as I minister the Gospel. Some people I talk to simply will not take any time at all to learn of Jesus. They reject him outright. Perhaps they are so far away from him they cannot even glimpse his magnificent light.

What do you do? The only thing you can do is keep talking about him. Some will listen. Some will not. There is nothing you can do about it. You can't force anyone to say, "I want Jesus." The Holy Spirit will do the convicting. Jesus wants you to do the telling. Why? Why doesn't the Spirit do the telling, too? After all, he moved to create the world. He can certainly create new believers.

Jesus invites you into the salvation process because it raises you up to see him more clearly. As you speak of him, the Spirit grows Jesus into your heart. The more you talk of Jesus, the more you will love him. He will get more and more real to you.

That's one reason Jesus sent the disciples to preach. Their words would bring others to faith. Their words would also grow up Jesus more and more in their hearts. That's why Jesus wants you to speak of him. Others need to know him. You will know him much more.

Pause and consider how speaking of Jesus is good for others and it's good for you.

A Good Place to Be

Time to Do

> *Mark 6:12-13 They went out and preached that people should repent. 13 They drove out many demons and anointed many sick people with oil and healed them. 14 King Herod heard about this, for Jesus' name had become well known. Some were saying, "John the Baptist has been raised from the dead, and that is why miraculous powers are at work in him."*

ARE YOU a "do-er"? You know, the kind of person who just gets at it, gets it done, figures it out as you go along, worrying little about planning but never ever planning to fail. There's always a way to succeed, isn't there?

There certainly is a way to succeed in the Kingdom of God. The success method is to be a "do-er" in the will of God under the power of God. You can easily see God's power on display here as the disciples preached the Gospel, healed the sick and drove out demons.

What happened? In their doing, Jesus' name became more well-known. As they ministered to save people in the name of the Savior, people in Galilee heard more and more of the Savior's work. From the lowliest peasant to the King Herod, Jesus name became known.

This is such a simple lesson. When you do as Jesus commands you, he will empower you to complete it. The Apostle Paul saw Jesus' power profoundly change his life, leading him to do good works for Jesus in many ways. As he proclaimed, *Philippians 1:6*
6 being confident of this, that he who began a good work in you will carry it on to completion until the day of Christ Jesus, he celebrated the work Jesus called him to do, and he celebrated that he had gone to do it.

Jesus called his disciples to be "do-ers", and the Gospel went forth into the world, into your hearts.

Pause and consider Jesus certainly wouldn't call his disciples to be "sitters".

Find Jesus Follow Jesus

It's True!

> Mark 6:16-18 But when Herod heard this, he said, "John, the man I beheaded, has been raised from the dead!" 17 For Herod himself had given orders to have John arrested, and he had him bound and put in prison. He did this because of Herodias, his brother Philip's wife, whom he had married. 18 For John had been saying to Herod, "It is not lawful for you to have your brother's wife."

THIS is weird. My wife just finished a conversation—I mean 10 seconds ago—about people stepping into new faith journeys with Jesus. The conversation closed with Barb saying, "Keep preaching the truth." And I said, "That's easy."

Then I read this.

Herod kills John for preaching the truth. Sin mocked salvation, and sin won. The Herald of the Christ is dead because he told the truth. Is it easy to preach the truth?

You bet. I'd rather die at the hand of a sinner than be condemned by the Savior into eternal death for denying his truth. You might ask, "Why would Jesus allow a sinner to kill a salvation messenger?" Go ahead, ask it, and here's what I tell you. "Every 'Why God?' question always points to this answer:

"God does everything for your good and for his glory."

No, John didn't end up "good" from our perspective, but he ended up "good" in Jesus perspective. He had completed his mission. He did as commanded. He told the truth, and today he's in the throne room of Heaven, "good" in the Lord.

What's more, Herod isn't "good". Herod's in hell. It is in God's glory that sin is eternally punished and the salvation messenger is eternally saved.

Yes, it *is* easy to preach the truth. The truth takes you to the "good" the eternal life.

Pause and consider brief or eternal good?

| A Good Place to Be

What Did He Hear?

> *Mark 6:19-20 So Herodias nursed a grudge against John and wanted to kill him. But she was not able to, 20 because Herod feared John and protected him, knowing him to be a righteous and holy man. When Herod heard John, he was greatly puzzled; yet he liked to listen to him.*

YOU SEE in this short account a man of power who had absolutely no power over evil. Herod Antipas was a king over Galilee and the area of the Decapolis. Galilee, of course, is the home territory of John the Baptist and Jesus. This is the same Herod whom Jesus is sent to at his "trial" on the day of his crucifixion.

Herod had great power to create beautiful gardens. He built cities and transformed ordinary villages into extraordinary visual splendor. He moved men and earth, but he couldn't move his heart to the right.

John preached to him—told him how evil he was to marry Herodias, his brother Philip's wife. John apparently had discussions with Herod. Herod "liked to listen to him", but Herod heard nothng he would like to do. Herod's desire was to please the sinful lusts of Herodias. Herod's desire was to please the sinful lusts of his heart. He heard the word of God, the Law of Moses, straight from the greatest prophet of all; yet, he said, "No thank you. This isn't for me."

It's easy to condemn him, isn't it? C'mon Herod, the word of God was right in your face! You denied it! You disdained it! You preferred your sinful heart over God's heart! You deserved to die for your sins, Herod!

Oh, wait a minute. What did I do about what God was saying to me in his Word today? What did I do about the sermon I heard last week? What did I do about *my* sin?

Pause and consider how you and I deserve to die for our sins, but Jesus died, instead.

Captivated With God

> Mark 6:21-23 *Finally the opportune time came. On his birthday Herod gave a banquet for his high officials and military commanders and the leading men of Galilee. 22 When the daughter of Herodias came in and danced, she pleased Herod and his dinner guests. The king said to the girl, "Ask me for anything you want, and I'll give it to you." 23 And he promised her with an oath, "Whatever you ask I will give you, up to half my kingdom."*

HEROD is so captivated with Herodias' daughter—actually his biological niece—that he is willing to give her half his kingdom. What kind of foolish, lustful man is this?

I'm afraid Herod's kind is much too common a kind of man. Sensual pleasure captivates the world. And fools rush after it. Does it captivate even you?

Before you answer, consider this: What are sins of the flesh? Could sins of the flesh be your desire for the newest car, latest tech tool, fanciest golf club, or extravagant clothes? Could sins of the flesh be too much TV or too much time on useless chatter in social networks? Could sins of the flesh be that morning "Starbucks"?

Think of Herod's lust. It captivated his soul until it destroyed him (He died in absolute, miserable exile). Now think about the things that captivate you. Are they the worldly things that will destroy you, exile you from friends and from God? Or are they things of God that will give you life with a loving relationship in Him and with others?

The Apostle Paul gives this advice: Colossians 2:8 *See to it that no one takes you captive through hollow and deceptive philosophy, which depends on human tradition and the basic principles of this world rather than on Christ.*

Pause and consider how captivating God's Word is to lead you to him.

| A Good Place to Be

God's Best Story

> *Mark 6:24-27 She went out and said to her mother, "What shall I ask for?" "The head of John the Baptist," she answered. 25 At once the girl hurried in to the king with the request: "I want you to give me right now the head of John the Baptist on a platter." 26 The king was greatly distressed, but because of his oaths and his dinner guests, he did not want to refuse her. 27 So he immediately sent an executioner with orders to bring John's head. The man went, beheaded John in the prison.*

YOU KNOW, sometimes it is really difficult reading the Bible. Here you have Evil in Herodias' daughter and Herod vs. Good in John the Baptist. And John is killed. This is really not fair, God. You created John to be a Messenger for the Christ. "Where are you in this, God? Why would John die?"

But then it's time to pause and consider how limited is my point-of-view. I see nothing of the future and how all matters must point to the New Heaven and Earth. Although it seems John's death and Herod's sin have no good purpose, you and I must understand that we do not understand everything God must do to complete his plan of saving us forever.

Throughout scripture there are some terribly difficult stories when evil seems to win. But remember that the worst of those stories is the beginning of the best of all stories.

Yes, evil seems to triumph over Good as Jesus is crucified. But God's plan for Jesus' death is for the beginning of your life. Jesus needed to die to conquer sin and Hell. Through God's worst story comes God's best story named Eternal Life.

Pause and consider how God's best story is for you.

Find Jesus Follow Jesus

Jesus Needed Rest

> Mark 6:30-32 *The apostles gathered around Jesus and reported to him all they had done and taught. 31 Then, because so many people were coming and going that they did not even have a chance to eat, he said to them, "Come with me by yourselves to a quiet place and get some rest." 32 So they went away by themselves in a boat to a solitary place.*

DO YOU get busy? Of course you do. Everyone has reasons to be busy. Jesus and his disciples had been plenty busy teaching and preaching God's Word, baptizing people, healing physical diseases, cleansing people of demonic possession and dealing with large crowds always pressing in on them. What should they do?

I love Jesus' solution: "Come with me by yourselves to a quiet place and get some rest." That's a great idea, isn't it? Or is it? Should Jesus and his disciples who had the ability to do so many wonderful stop to rest? After all, there are things to do. There people to save. How could Jesus suggest they stop?

He could suggest the stopping because they needed to prepare for their next "going". In order to minister, they needed physical rest and spiritual renewal. After all God created the body to rest every day. And God created the soul to seek him every day. To minister in power, Jesus and his disciples needed physical rest and soul nourishing.

Guess what? You are the same. You need these, too, every day. If you respond, "I'm too busy to be quiet and rest. I'm too busy to take time for God's Word." I'll say, "No, you're not. Jesus needed this in his humanity. So do you."

Pause and consider how good it is too rest and feel God's care.

A Good Place to Be

Jesus, the Changer

> *Mark 6:33 But many who saw them leaving recognized them and ran on foot from all the towns and got there ahead of them.*

DO YOU ever run after Jesus?

Look at these people. They are running on foot to get to Jesus' next preaching and healing place. They are excited! They know what Jesus can do, and they want to see it again. They want to experience Jesus again.

But you're not like that are you? You think, "Maybe I should spend some time in prayer today." But then you look at the calendar, realize you have all these things to do and you just don't have time for prayer, Bible study or for Jesus. How about your kids? Are they too busy with school, their sport leagues or having friends over to have time for Jesus?

Instead of running to Jesus you run away from Jesus. You try hard to avoid him because you know what he can do. He can change you.

That's why the people ran ahead of Jesus. They saw Jesus change lives, and they desperately desired Jesus to change their lives. They knew if he spoke to them they would be different. They knew if he touched them they would be different. They *wanted* the change, a new life.

Why don't you? I mean, why do you want to keep hating someone who hurt you? Why do you keep speaking in ways that hurts others? Why can't you speak love to your spouse? Why can't you put your children above your material desires? Why do you always say, "Not now." when the church announces the next series of Bible studies?

What is so good about your life you don't want Jesus to change you?

Pause and consider the change Jesus offers you—every bit of it is good for you.

Find Jesus Follow Jesus

A Good Teacher

> Mark 6:34 When Jesus landed and saw a large crowd, he had compassion on them, because they were like sheep without a shepherd. So he began teaching them many things.

WHEN YOU think of the most influential people in your life who is on that list? Would you include someone who has taught you or mentored you? Likely you would. Hardly any one of us is who we are without the aid of a good teacher.

Here is Jesus being a good teacher and forming the lives of the 12 disciples. Can you consider some of the "many things" he taught them? Certainly they would be the holy ways of God. He taught them with words that would form and shape their minds. Hearing his love, their hearts would begin to re-form into hearts of love. Knowing his forgiveness, their minds would be open to forgiving others. Hearing the absolute truth from the Way, the Truth and the Life would certainly be a life-forming experience wouldn't it? Certainly Jesus would be on the disciples' list as the most influential person in their lives.

I pray that this is true for you. As you live your life and wonder, "What's right? What do I do now? How can I forgive that person? How can I love that person? How can I live a good life?" Please know you have the same transforming, life-shaping teacher as the disciples.

Think of that: You have the same transforming, life-shaping teacher as the disciples.

He's there on your coffee table or on your bookcase. He's there in the desk. He's there in the Holy Bible.

Open it and receive the teaching. Jesus must be the most important "person" who shapes your life.

Pause and consider why would you not want the Resurrection and the Life to be your teacher?

A Good Place to Be

You Feed Them

> *Mark 6:35-37 By this time it was late in the day, so his disciples came to him. "This is a remote place," they said, "and it's already very late. 36 Send the people away so they can go to the surrounding countryside and villages and buy themselves something to eat." 37 But he answered, "You give them something to eat." They said to him, "That would take eight months of a man's wages! Are we to go and spend that much on bread and give it to them to eat?"*

DOES GOD'S word feed you?

Sometimes in the church, people gather in smaller groups for years to study God's Word. They like being "fed" in God's truth this way, and so they should.

But too often the group members are reluctant to leave the group and start to feed new people in God's Word. It's a hard thing, isn't it, to go from the table where you're being fed to a place where you have to do the feeding? Often the question is, "If I'm being fed, God's Word, why should I leave the source of my food?"

The answer to that question is in this scripture. When the disciples are concerned about the people eating, he says, *"You give them something to eat."* Why?

Jesus wanted his disciples to act in the power of God's Word to feed a meal to the crowd. He had been feeding God's Truth to them to fill them with the Word of God to act in the power of God's Word, and now it's time to do God's Word.

Why should Bible study members leave the "table" and go to feed others? As Jesus prepared his disciples, God's Word has prepared them to act in God's Word and feed the world.

Pause and consider God's Word is to feed you that you may feed others.

Find Jesus Follow Jesus

Go Sit Down

> Mark 6:38-39 *"How many loaves do you have?" he asked. "Go and see." When they found out, they said, "Five — and two fish." 39 Then Jesus directed them to have all the people sit down in groups on the green grass.*

DO YOU think living the Christian life requires that you are busy doing many things? After all, a big part of Jesus' teaching is to *do* things that make a difference in your own and others' lives. And certainly, if you belong to a church, you often hear, "Get involved! Serve the poor. Teach a class."

The doing is necessary and vital to spread the Gospel to others. But sometimes it's good to go and sit down.

Jesus had just finished speaking to thousands of people. "Church" was just over. Jesus and his leadership team had a quick meeting: The disciples essentially said, "There's neither food nor money." Jesus said, "You feed them."

Instead of turning the crowd away because it was "impossible" to do what they desired, instead of tabling the discussion for another time, Jesus acted in faith of what the Father would provide him and the crowd.

Jesus dismissed the meeting. He said, "Go sit down." to the crowd. And he told his leaders to pass out a few fish and loaves. The disciples faithfully did the work. The Son blessed the meal. The Father provided. The crowd ate.

Sometimes you are the leader to direct the doing. Sometimes you are the worker to do the action. Sometimes you go sit down, and you receive blessings of the doing. That's the proper Christian life. That's the balanced Christian life.

Go to the Master, and he will direct you to what to do—sometimes to even sit down.

Pause and consider that sitting with God is good time to be filled with God.

A Good Place to Be

A Filling Meal

> *Mark 6:40 So they sat down in groups of hundreds and fifties. 41 Taking the five loaves and the two fish and looking up to heaven, Jesus gave thanks and broke the loaves. Then he gave them to his disciples to set before the people. He also divided the two fish among them all. 42 They all ate and were satisfied, 43 and the disciples picked up twelve basketfuls of broken pieces of bread and fish.*

JESUS feeds the 5,000. You've probably read and heard this story often, haven't you? You've also heard of "Jesus saves". Do you see how this magnificent miracle of "Jesus feeds the 5,000" is the perfect picture of the miracle "Jesus saves"?

On that day thousands have come to hear Jesus teach the true word of God. They are hungry to know: Is God's word real for me? As Jesus teaches the Word, it begins to fill them. As a nourishing meal to the stomach is life to the body, the Living Word is life to the soul. After their meal, their stomachs are full. When Jesus' teaching is done, their spirits, too are filled.

All of this happens only in the power of God. The literal food multiplies as Jesus prays to the Father. God's Word multiplies as you pray for ears to hear and minds to know.

The miracle of the food is life to the body. The miracle of God's Word taught is life to the soul.

Pause and consider: *Isaiah 55:11 so is my word that goes out from my mouth: It will not return to me empty, but will accomplish what I desire and achieve the purpose for which I sent it.*

Find Jesus Follow Jesus

Time for "Thank You"

> Mark 6:45-46 *Immediately Jesus made his disciples get into the boat and go on ahead of him to Bethsaida, while he dismissed the crowd. 46 After leaving them, he went up on a mountainside to pray.*

YOU have seen before in Mark's Gospel how Jesus got up early in the morning to pray before he began his work for the day. In this scene today, you see that Jesus work is done. And there he goes again, off alone to pray. Although you aren't told what Jesus prays here, his prayer focus could be determined from the day's events.

How do you respond when some really good things occur in your life? Do you say, "Thank you." to people who have helped those things happen? Do you, perhaps say, "Thank you, Father for the good things that happened today."

That easily could have been Jesus' prayer. Perhaps as many as 10,000 people came to hear him that day (Scripture records 5,000 men, and then you add women and children.). Certainly it is the Father in the power of the Holy Spirit who moved people's hearts to hear Jesus' preaching.

Those thousands were fed with a very tiny food source. Certainly it is the Father in the power of the Holy Spirit who multiplied the loaves and fish. Jesus' disciples, too, had learned a powerful lesson about their rabbi and about their God. Yes, certainly Jesus' prayer time that evening included a time of praise and thanksgiving to God.

On this day, what is a good thing to include in your prayers? Certainly there are issues in your life and/or lives of loved ones that are difficult to deal with. But remember the reasons you have to say to the Father, "Thank you for the …." Pray thanksgiving, and praise the Father.

Pause and consider that "Thank You!" is pleasing to God.

A Good Place to Be

More to Know

> *Mark 6:47-50 When evening came, the boat was in the middle of the lake, and he was alone on land. 48 He saw the disciples straining at the oars, because the wind was against them. About the fourth watch of the night he went out to them, walking on the lake. He was about to pass by them, 49 but when they saw him walking on the lake, they thought he was a ghost. They cried out, 50 because they all saw him and were terrified. Immediately he spoke to them and said, "Take courage! It is I. Don't be afraid."*

DO YOU ever think, "I don't know enough about Jesus." Be assured, you're not alone. Even the disciples who walked "in his dust" had much to learn about Jesus.

Jesus has driven demons from crazy men. He has raised a dead girl to life. He has stilled the storms with a word. He has fed over 5,000 people. And now he walks on water.

I've often wondered why Jesus did this. Didn't he do enough miracles without this one that scared his disciples? Here are two reasons I think Jesus walked on water.

First, he *did* have to further demonstrate his power. His disciples had doubted his ability to feed the thousands. They had not even considered his power when they exclaimed, "That would take 8 months' wages!" as they thought of buying food to obey Jesus' command, "You give them something to eat."

Second, there's Job 9:8 *He alone stretches out the heavens and treads on the waves of the sea.* God's Word says only God has the power to walk on water. Jesus is showing his disciples he is the sovereign Lord of the universe.

Jesus clearly shows he is God. Do you see him?

Pause and consider Jesus' power to save is all around you.

Find Jesus Follow Jesus

Get Real

> Mark 7:5-8 *So the Pharisees and teachers of the law asked Jesus, "Why don't your disciples live according to the tradition of the elders instead of eating their food with 'unclean' hands?" 6 He replied, "Isaiah was right when he prophesied about you hypocrites; as it is written: "'These people honor me with their lips, but their hearts are far from me. 7 They worship me in vain; their teachings are but rules taught by men.' 8 You have let go of the commands of God and are holding on to the traditions of men."*

DO YOU wash before you eat? That wasn't a habit in Jesus' day, unless you were a Pharisee.

They had what looks to us like a good "tradition of the elders". They washed before they ate! But when they criticized the disciples, they were concerned only about the disciples' rule following.

Their question disturbed Jesus. He knew that, although the Pharisees washed on the outside, they had plenty of dirt on their hearts. Their actions were to make themselves look good before others and had nothing to do with worshiping God.

Jesus gets really angry with these "unreal" Pharisees. They had the knowledge of God's law, a law that focused on loving God and loving others. Yet, they created and lived in laws that were about loving themselves.

Do you get "lawful" about your relationship with God? Some Christians dress a certain way. Some reject certain foods. Some refuse to forgive a broken child. Some judge others before cleaning up their own lives. Such unreal actions can cause you to say, "Look at me."

Be careful what you do. Be sure your actions point to God, not you.

Pause and consider God's ways are the way to Him.

A Good Place to Be

Scrawling a Whim

> Mark 7:9-13 He went on, "Well, good for you. You get rid of God's command so you won't be inconvenienced in following the religious fashions! 10 Moses said, 'Respect your father and mother,' and, 'Anyone denouncing father or mother should be killed.' 11 But you weasel out of that by saying that it's perfectly acceptable to say to father or mother, 'Gift?! What I owed you I've given as a gift to God,' 12 thus relieving yourselves of obligation to father or mother. 13 You scratch out God's Word and scrawl a whim in its place. You do a lot of things like this." (from THE MESSAGE)

WHAT DO you think of the phrase *"you scrawl a whim in its place"*? Today I heard of a church denomination that allows its pastors to stay at a church for only 18 months. My questions to this church are: "Did you scrawl a whim over God's Word?" limiting your pastors to service? I hope they haven't. Jesus would be most displeased with that.

Yes, Jesus hates the way mankind has "scrawled a whim" to override God's Word. How dare we form our own understanding of God apart from his Word? God's Word is as a love letter to you. He has formed his Word for the benefit of communicating to you that he *loves you*. Yet, you and I too often live in doubt and ambivalence of his Word. And worse, we live with an attitude that *our words* are better than God's Word.

That's the Pharisees' sin. They had put their own word over God's Word, and Jesus condemned them for "scrawling their whim" on God's law.

Love and honor God's Word. He has written it for you.

Pause and consider how you wouldn't scrawl over a love note to you.

Real is Jesus-Like

> Mark 7:14-15 *Again Jesus called the crowd to him and said, "Listen to me, everyone, and understand this. 15 Nothing outside a man can make him 'unclean' by going into him. Rather, it is what comes out of a man that makes him 'unclean.'"*

HOW DO you like change? I remember working with teens many years ago. Teens are supposed to want things to be different than their parents. They like new ways of doing things, right? I'm not sure. The teens I worked with seemed reluctant to change to anything new. They liked what they knew.

The truth is, we all like what we know. But Jesus had come to change the world into God's ways of grace. You will see in the Old Testament Law that God instructed his people to not eat certain foods. This food restriction was for a purpose as God formed his people. Now God has a new purpose—to change all mankind into one people. Jesus begins the change by removing the Jews' diet restrictions.

When he says, *"Nothing outside a man can make him 'unclean' by going into him."* he is saying that it is okay to eat the foods and grains of creation. He's also saying this: What you say and what you do is what really makes you clean or unclean before God.

The Jews didn't like to hear this change. Change meant leaving behind something sacred to them. That's why change is hard—we hold sacred our habits, even when they're not. Yet Jesus insists the Jews change their hearts and habits to consume God's Word, and that would be enough.

Pause and consider what you consume—does it honor God?

A Good Place to Be

One More Time

> Mark 7:17-20 *After he had left the crowd and entered the house, his disciples asked him about this parable. 18 "Are you so dull?" he asked. "Don't you see that nothing that enters a man from the outside can make him 'unclean'? 19 For it doesn't go into his heart but into his stomach, and then out of his body." (In saying this, Jesus declared all foods "clean.")*

DON'T YOU get it? Jesus said it. Why isn't it clear to you?

Do you walk out of a sermon, a Bible study, or close this email and ask, "What was that about?" I hope not. But I have to believe that sometimes you do.

The truth is, sometimes the truth is hard to hear. You hear the words as you read or someone speaks them clearly, but you don't "hear" their meaning. The Bible is not always easy to understand. So what do you do?

You do what the disciples do. You ask a question or two, or three. The disciples needed to ask their rabbi questions, so they could thoroughly understand him. But why is it Jesus seems to be "short" with them? Why the question, "Why are you so dull?"

The thing is, Jesus really, really needs his disciples to know the truth. They are being taught as no one has ever been taught before. It is critical they get it. If they mess up the truth, God's Word you and I will never know it. He's calling them to account in their earthly life because they will have to account to him one day in their eternal life.

Are you confused about the Bible? Then find a way to know it. Jesus will also hold you to an account of the truth one day.

Pause and consider that dull is no part of the Light of the Word.

Sin Defined

> Mark 7:21-23 *For from within, out of men's hearts, come evil thoughts, sexual immorality, theft, murder, adultery, 22 greed, malice, deceit, lewdness, envy, slander, arrogance and folly. 23 All these evils come from inside and make a man 'unclean'.*

NOW YOU know. Jesus labels sin "unclean".

How often we minimize sin. "Adultery" is sexual freedom. "Folly" is, "I deserve to have some fun." "Lewdness" is, "That's the language of the day." "Sexual immorality" is, "Born that way."

Yes, we're born that way. You and I are born into the ways of evil, but we have other words to define evil. "Choice" "rights" "freedom" are a few words we use to hide the evil in our hearts from our own consciousness. We are sinners who are far short of the glory God has intended for our lives.

So what do you do? The Bible is clear. First, you tell God point blank with words from your heart, "I confess, Lord that I have _____." You say it. You might even write it down to make it real. You'll be amazed how quickly you will want to let go of that sin. It becomes too real to keep.

Then even more real for you is Jesus' death for you. That's what you do second. You tell Jesus, "Thank you, Jesus, for dying for me. I was so dirty, and you made me so clean. Forgive me, Lord Jesus. Rescue me from my sins."

Third, you put this sin list someplace you can easily see it. You remember it. This list will keep your choices clear. Your good choice will keep your heart clear.

Pause and consider how clearly the list defines sin. You have no reason to say, "I didn't know."

A Good Place to Be

Just a Crumb

> Mark 7:24-29 Jesus left that place and went to the vicinity of Tyre. He entered a house and did not want anyone to know it; yet he could not keep his presence secret. 25 In fact, as soon as she heard about him, a woman whose little daughter was possessed by an evil spirit came and fell at his feet. 26 The woman was a Greek, born in Syrian Phoenicia. She begged Jesus to drive the demon out of her daughter. 27 "First let the children eat all they want," he told her, "for it is not right to take the children's bread and toss it to their dogs." 28 "Yes, Lord," she replied, "but even the dogs under the table eat the children's crumbs." 29 Then he told her, "For such a reply, you may go; the demon has left your daughter."

IF YOU have a dog and a small child in the house, you notice how quickly the dog learns to get next to the child at meal time. The dog knows crumbs will fall, and he will eat.

Do you know to go next to Jesus? Jesus of Nazareth is "feeding" his people with healing and salvation when they come to him in faith. Thus came the Greek woman desperate for her daughter. She came knowing that if Jesus offered her even a "scrap" of his power, her daughter would be healed.

Jesus responds, "First let he children eat all they want" as he refers to the Jews receiving his healing. But fully trusting the power of Jesus she asks for just a crumb. And that crumb was enough of Jesus to heal her daughter.

Pause and consider is your faith big enough to require only a little of Jesus?

Find Jesus Follow Jesus

Why the Sigh?

> Mark 7:31-34 Then Jesus left the vicinity of Tyre and went through Sidon, down to the Sea of Galilee and into the region of the Decapolis. 32 There some people brought to him a man who was deaf and could hardly talk, and they begged him to place his hand on the man. 33 After he took him aside, away from the crowd, Jesus put his fingers into the man's ears. Then he spit and touched the man's tongue. 34 He looked up to heaven and with a deep sigh said to him, "Ephphatha!" (which means, "Be opened!"). 5 At this, the man's ears were opened, his tongue was loosened and he began to speak plainly.

WHY DO you think Mark records that Jesus emitted a deep sigh at this healing? Could Jesus as the divine Son of Man, who is coming to judge the world one day, be considering at this moment how broken his world is? Could he be sighing over the overwhelming darkness, sickness, faithlessness and weakness that dominate mankind?

In his sighing, Jesus could be expressing a weariness of his soul for your sake. As a parent you may sigh over the hard things a child faces because someone has hurt him. You feel weary because your child is broken.

Jesus felt the pain of his people's brokenness. And you can be grateful that he did and he does. He loves you so much he desires your health of body, mind and soul. When sin attacks you, he hurts for you, and he longs to heal you.

Jesus' sighing is a symptom of his love and compassion for you. Be glad the Lord has sighed. Rejoice his nail-driven hands now touch your soul to heal you.

Pause and consider Jesus' deep sigh is a sign of his deep love.

A Good Place to Be

What's a Command?

> Mark 7:36-37 Jesus commanded them not to tell anyone. But the more he did so, the more they kept talking about it. 37 People were overwhelmed with amazement. "He has done everything well," they said. "He even makes the deaf hear and the mute speak."

"**WHAT IS** *wrong with you?* Don't you ever *listen* to anything I say?"

You probably have heard that from someone who has asked you, told you, even commanded you to do something. You didn't do what you were commanded to do, and the person was completely frustrated with you. After all, isn't the only appropriate response to an appropriate command to *do it?*

But that's not mankind's response to the commands of the Holy Trinity. Do you see what happened when "*Jesus commanded them not to tell anyone*"? What did "they" do? "T*he more he (commanded them to not tell); the more they kept talking about it."*

What is humanity's problem, anyway? Why are we so disobedient? Jesus often gives this command when he heals, and every time he does, people disobey him and talk about it. Is it not cause to wonder why Jesus continued his work to save such a disobedient people?

But isn't that true of history? From the very beginning, God commanded Adam and Eve to not eat the forbidden fruit. They disobeyed. God gave the Hebrews the Ten Commandments. They disobeyed. The prophets commanded God's people to repent. The people disobeyed. Jesus came to command His people to believe His Good News. The people disobeyed. Now the Spirit of God comes to command to you the truth of God's Word.

What do *you do*?

Pause and consider: there's only one appropriate response to God's commands.

Practical Compassion

> Mark 8:1-3 During those days another large crowd gathered. Since they had nothing to eat, Jesus called his disciples to him and said, 2 "I have compassion for these people; they have already been with me three days and have nothing to eat. 3 If I send them home hungry, they will collapse on the way, because some of them have come a long distance."

YOU'VE been around practical, compassionate people haven't you? You know, she's the mom who loves to make sure you have plenty to eat. He's the dad who takes all the kids to the game and is willing to stop for a pizza afterward. She's the one who stops by with a casserole when you're sick. He's the one willing to fix your leaky faucet. Their help is practical because it's for your everyday needs. Their help is compassionate because they convey a clear sense of desiring to help you.

Practical compassion is certainly what your Lord Jesus displays here. Repeating a scene found in Mark 6, thousands have come to hear him. Perhaps they had brought food with them. But the preaching and teaching was long. The food is gone. What will your Lord do?

He will feed them, of course. Why not? He can because it's the practical thing to do, and he has the power to do so. He will because he has compassion on them. He will not let them leave hungry, at risk of becoming ill.

Often we think it's only appropriate to pray to Jesus when we need big things. Everything—even lunch—is a big thing for Jesus because it is his practical compassionate way to care for you.

Pause and consider Jesus loves you—and wants to care for your every need.

A Good Place to Be

"But That Was Yesterday"

> Mark 8:4 His disciples answered, "But where in this remote place can anyone get enough bread to feed them?"

HAVE YOU in any way ever experienced the wonder of Jesus' love for you? Perhaps it was a simple touch of love from a pastor, a parent, or a friend at a moment when you needed to absolutely know that at least *one* person loved you. What was it like? Did it fill you with gratitude for the one who touched you? For Jesus?

What happened the next time you needed that kind of loving touch? Did you wonder, "Does anyone love me?" Did you possibly forget about the first time? Or did you feel, "But that was yesterday." doubting that Jesus would show up again?

That seems to be the disciples' issue here. They had seen and helped Jesus feed thousands of people from a few loaves and fish. Now there's another hungry crowd, and the disciples wonder, "Where's the food coming from?"

Did you forget, Mr. Disciples, how lovingly your Lord fed "the 5,000"? Or did you think "But that was yesterday." and surely Jesus won't use all his "feeding power" again. Did you feel his compassion for the hungry crowds was depleted?

Yet, he fed them, didn't he? Even without the disciples' faith to ask, "Will you feed these as you fed the others?" Jesus fed them. He fed them because he cared for them. He fed them to demonstrate to the disciples once again his power to feed.

They would need many times in their future to know their Lord's power. Perhaps they would remember this day and trust Jesus to "feed them" in their need.

Pause and consider Jesus' has constant power to feed you his love.

Good to Focus

> Mark 8:5-9 *"How many loaves do you have?" Jesus asked. "Seven," they replied. 6 He told the crowd to sit down on the ground. When he had taken the seven loaves and given thanks, he broke them and gave them to his disciples to set before the people, and they did so. 7 They had a few small fish as well; he gave thanks for them also and told the disciples to distribute them. 8 The people ate and were satisfied. Afterward the disciples picked up seven basketfuls of broken pieces that were left over. 9 About four thousand men were present.*

YOU usually focus on Jesus' actions here, don't you? Of course you do as you should. But let's focus for a moment on the disciples' actions.

How does Jesus involve them in his miracle? First, he asks them, "How many loaves do you have?" Why would he ask them something he would know (He is good at doing this.)? He wants them to focus on how little they have. He wants them to say, "Seven.", so they will focus on it.

Then the disciples distribute the food. Why? Practically speaking, who else would do it? It's an orderly process. But something else is going on here. As the disciples hand out the bread, they are piece-by-piece focusing on the Lord's multiplying power. The same happens as they distribute the fish.

Then do you see what the disciples do? They *pick up the leftovers*! Why? Again it's practical. Again, it's to focus on the truth that they had more after the meal than they had before the meal.

Do you think the disciples could now more faithfully focus on Jesus' multiplying power?

Pause and consider how Jesus' multiplying power is still available for you.

| A Good Place to Be

"If You're Real, Lord!"

> Mark 8:10-13 he got into the boat with his disciples and went to the region of Dalmanutha. 11 The Pharisees came and began to question Jesus. To test him, they asked him for a sign from heaven. 12 He sighed deeply and said, "Why does this generation ask for a miraculous sign? I tell you the truth, no sign will be given to it." 13 Then he left them, got back into the boat and crossed to the other side.

DID YOU ever try to bargain with God? You know the deal: "If you're real, Jesus, you'll heal my blindness." You'll cure my wife's cancer. You'll fix my finances, Jesus. Just do this one thing, and I'll believe in you. I'll even go to church once…or twice."

What's wrong with that? What's wrong with the Pharisees testing Jesus and asking for a "sign from heaven"? Glad you asked.

The truth is, the Pharisees have no intention of turning their faith to Jesus regardless of what he does. They are there to "test" God. God does not allow you to test him. He is not a butler waiting for you to ring his bell. God alone is God. A "faith" based on one response from God is no faith. God cannot possibly function as the Sovereign Lord, if he has to prove himself to you.

It's easy isn't it, to want the Lord to show up in just the way you desire? God calls you, though, to trust him to offer to you—even blindness, illness or difficult times—for His good purposes to save the world from Hell.

The cross and the empty tomb are the only signs you need to know from Jesus. Receive them and be saved.

Pause and consider the signs of life Jesus offers to you.

The Third Time?

> Mark 8:14-15 *The disciples had forgotten to bring bread, except for one loaf they had with them in the boat. 15 "Be careful," Jesus warned them. "Watch out for the yeast of the Pharisees and that of Herod."*

DO YOU see the disciples worry here? Although not explicitly stated, they are short of bread on their trip. They are in charge of the food supplies, and they realize they have failed to bring enough food for their time to the eastern side of the Sea of Galilee.

What do you think? Should they be worried? Twice they have watched and participated in Jesus feeding thousands of people from a few loaves of bread. Why worry? Jesus can feed thousands. He can certainly feed a dozen or so.

Yes, there is something wrong with the disciples. They still only "half believe" Jesus' power is always available to care for them. As Jesus warns them *"Watch out for the yeast of the Pharisees and that of Herod."* he is referring to the sin of these people. The sin of the authorities in Galilee is they do not believe in Jesus. They have denied him. They have criticized Jesus, they have felt threatened by Jesus, and they have shown no faith in him.

"Be careful," Jesus says. "You don't want that sin in your heart. Focus on me." In Luke 12:29-30 Jesus teaches them: *And do not set your heart on what you will eat or drink; do not worry about it. 30 For the pagan world runs after all such things, and your Father knows that you need them."*

Trust in the power of God to provide for your needs, and be content with what you have.

Pause and consider how content you will be trusting God's care for you.

A Good Place to Be

Feeling Uncomfortable?

> Mark 8:16-21 *They discussed this with one another and said, "It is because we have no bread." 17 Aware of their discussion, Jesus asked them: "Why are you talking about having no bread? Do you still not see or understand? Are your hearts hardened? 18 Do you have eyes but fail to see, and ears but fail to hear? And don't you remember? 19 When I broke the five loaves for the five thousand, how many basketfuls of pieces did you pick up?" "Twelve," they replied. 20 "And when I broke the seven loaves for the four thousand, how many basketfuls of pieces did you pick up?" They answered, "Seven." 21 He said to them, "Do you still not understand?"*

HAVE you ever been in a meeting or classroom or even church when someone reprimanded you for not "getting it"? They had told you how to do something. They had watched you do it. They had even helped you do it, but you still did not understand what you were being taught. Somehow, some way, you just didn't get it. You were probably embarrassed weren't you?

When I've been in that situation, I try to blame someone or something else. "You didn't say it clearly. I had too much to do. I was tired. I was too busy to learn it." We're always making excuses for not learning something, not "getting it" aren't we?

The real truth is, though, you and I must understand Jesus' teachings. We must pay attention to the One who died for us and who rose again that we might be saved. One day you will stand before him, and you certainly don't want him saying to you, *"Do you still not understand?"*

Pause and consider you must know Jesus' eternal truth.

Find Jesus Follow Jesus

A Seeing Lesson

> Mark 8:22-25 *They came to Bethsaida, and some people brought a blind man and begged Jesus to touch him. 23 He took the blind man by the hand and led him outside the village. When he had spit on the man's eyes and put his hands on him, Jesus asked, "Do you see anything?" 24 He looked up and said, "I see people; they look like trees walking around." 25 Once more Jesus put his hands on the man's eyes. Then his eyes were opened, his sight was restored, and he saw everything clearly.*

WHAT DO you see about this miracle that is different than any other Jesus does? He heals in two stages, doesn't he? And he forms mud from his own spit to place on the man's eyes. Why might his purpose be for this type of healing?

Could this healing be a demonstration to the disciples once more of his efforts to get them to see who he is? He has been struggling to teach them that he is trustworthy, that they can call on him for their "daily bread", and that he is the source of all life. Time and again he has given to them opportunities to experience (Luke 4:18) "*recovery of sight for the blind*" as he teaches them Kingdom truths.

Jesus takes the man to a quiet place. The disciples watch. They hear Jesus ask, "Do you see anything." The blind man responds with the beginning of sight. Then the healing is complete with Jesus' second touch. Do you think the disciples might have seen themselves as the blind man, gradually gaining a clear vision of Jesus?

When reading and hearing God's Word, do you see anything? Do you see it is for you?

Pause and consider how God's Word gives you clear eyes to see Jesus.

A Good Place to Be

Who Is He?

> Mark 8:27-29 Jesus and his disciples went on to the villages around Caesarea Philippi. On the way he asked them, "Who do people say I am?" 28 They replied, "Some say John the Baptist; others say Elijah; and still others, one of the prophets." 29 "But what about you?" he asked. "Who do you say I am?" Peter answered, "You are the Christ."

I COULD easily ask you, "Who do you say Jesus is?" but I won't. Why not? I want you to stop and consider Jesus and your answer for a while—perhaps a week or so, maybe even longer. And I'm hoping you'll come up with the answers that will honor Jesus. (Perhaps you can email me a note when you've considered your answer.)

In your consideration, be careful of your own thoughts. In other words, Peter rightly answered Jesus by saying, "You are the Christ." But does Peter fully know what that means? To the Jew, the Christ is an earthly ruler releasing them from foreign rule. Peter would come to know the Christ's fullness when he saw his resurrected body and when Jesus fed him breakfast along the sea, calling him to "feed my sheep". (See John 21.) He'd know Jesus even more when he began preaching, healing and then dying for his Lord.

Thus, when I ask you to spend some time answering the question, "Who do you say Jesus is?" I'd like you to go beyond your mind to consider what Scripture says about him, what your experiences are with him and what you feel as you read Scripture.

For example, if you call him, "Savior." will you live a life feeling joy and peace, assured and grateful that he has saved you to eternal life?

Pause and consider that, "How do you see Jesus?" requires an appropriate response.

Tough Teacher

> Mark 8:31-33 He then began to teach them that the Son of Man must suffer many things and be rejected by the elders, chief priests and teachers of the law, and that he must be killed and after three days rise again. 32 He spoke plainly about this, and Peter took him aside and began to rebuke him. 33 But when Jesus turned and looked at his disciples, he rebuked Peter. "Get behind me, Satan!" he said. "You do not have in mind the things of God, but the things of men."

WHEN Peter comes to Jesus to passionately rebuke Jesus for saying he must die, Jesus calls Peter, "Satan." How can the tender, merciful and loving Lord Jesus respond so harshly to the disciple who desired to protect him?

God has chosen Peter for a magnificent work in the Kingdom of God. (Matthew 16:18) *"You are Peter, and on this rock I will build my church, and the gates of Hell will not overcome it."*

Peter, Hell itself will strive against you to stop your appointed mission on earth. Hell is influencing you to try to stop Jesus' mission to the cross. Do not let Hell prevail, Peter. Call on the Lord.

Please, Peter, look past the part about Jesus dying and look to the part of his promise to "after three days rise again". Take your eyes from your worldly limitations and look to the power of Jesus to overcome Hell.

Jesus needed to be tough on you that day, Peter, to awaken you to the powerful Hellish forces against you. He needed you to claim for the rest of your life the most powerful Heavenly forces for your earthly ministry.

Pause and consider: call on Heavne's power to turn away Hell.

A Good Place to Be

A Cross?

> Mark 8:34-37 Then he called the crowd to him along with his disciples and said: "If anyone would come after me, he must deny himself and take up his cross and follow me. 35 For whoever wants to save his life will lose it, but whoever loses his life for me and for the gospel will save it. 36 What good is it for a man to gain the whole world, yet forfeit his soul? 37 Or what can a man give in exchange for his soul?

YOU and I really have no idea how horrible the cross is. You can read of its terrible affects on the human body and know the cross was an execution reserved for the worst criminals. But you and I have never watched a man horribly die on a cross.

The people of Jesus' day knew the cross. How do you, then, think they responded when Jesus spoke his cross-picking-up words? Certainly they said, "What? Take up my cross, Jesus? Does that mean I have to die a horrible death if I follow you?"

But then Jesus in effect says, "Even if it is excruciating to let go of the things you love, the things you are most passionate about, the things you think are important, you will eternally die."

Yes, following Jesus is about dying to your own will. And sometimes, as many martyrs have experienced through the ages, following Jesus means dying a physical death.

Why? Why is the Gospel so important that Jesus had to take up his cross and that you have to take up your cross?

Is anything more important than your eternal life?

Pause and consider the cause of heaven is above all causes.

Find Jesus Follow Jesus

Stand for Jesus

> Mark 8:38 *If anyone is ashamed of me and my words in this adulterous and sinful generation, the Son of Man will be ashamed of him when he comes in his Father's glory with the holy angels."*

WHY would anyone be ashamed of the Good News of Jesus Christ? The Apostle Paul says this (Romans 1:16) *I am not ashamed of the gospel, because it is the power of God for the salvation of everyone who believes: first for the Jew, then for the Gentile.*

He wasn't ashamed to preach, teach and evangelize the Gospel to unbelievers. He knew the power of the Gospel to save. Do you?

I think your shame level relates to your faith level. How faithfully do you believe the Gospel is the power to save people from sin's devastation?

Some of us have been blessed to be raised in a Gospel-preaching church, and we have come to accept the Gospel. Then we look at a world of people who act so violently against the Gospel, and we wonder, "How can any words I say, even God's words, change them?"

Some of you have lived very hard lives, and the Gospel *has saved* you! But then you doubt that it will save anyone else. We in the church are so reluctant, bashful and ashamed to tell the Gospel to the unsaved soul because we are not absolutely convinced "*it is the power of God for the salvation of everyone who believes*".

Why not? Don't we trust God to do what he says he will? Don't we trust that the Gospel will work in other souls as it has in ours? It's time to put aside your shame and start believing.

Pause and consider: What will Jesus say about your faith?

A Good Place to Be

Kingdom Power

> Mark 9:1 And he said to them, "I tell you the truth, some who are standing here will not taste death before they see the kingdom of God come with power."

WHAT DO you think about the phrase "kingdom of God come with power"? Is that the end of time when Jesus returns? Is it the beginning of the Church at Pentecost? Certainly it can be and is both. But could Jesus have been talking about the moment at hand with his disciples? This verse could easily be a bridge between Jesus' discussion of the Son of Man coming in power and glory at the end of Chapter 8, and Jesus' transfiguration in Mark 9:2-3.

You could say, "The power show is ramping up." Mark 9 is the beginning of Jesus' final journey to the cross. He has much left to show and tell his disciples. One of the things he has to show "some" of them—i.e. Peter, James and John, is a spectacular view of his heavenly glory.

As this favored threesome see Jesus transfigured before their eyes, they will see the glory of the Kingdom of God come to earth. Jesus' power overwhelms them. Peter dumbly responds, and Jesus' glory is gone.

But then Peter and John are the first disciples to see the empty tomb—the power of the Kingdom of God demonstrated in Jesus' resurrection. They were key to beginning the church. They saw the power of the Kingdom of God in the salvation of thousands of people in the early years of the church.

God shows his Kingdom power in many life-changing ways. See the power in God's Word and in your life. And be ready for the day you will see the Kingdom power coming on the clouds.

Pause and consider the kingdom power is Jesus' power to save and to judge.

Transfigured

> Mark 9:2-3 After six days Jesus took Peter, James and John with him and led them up a high mountain, where they were all alone. There he was transfigured before them. 3 His clothes became dazzling white, whiter than anyone in the world could bleach them.

HAVE YOU thought about "transfigured"? It means *"to transform one's appearance revealing great beauty and magnificence."* That's what happened to Jesus that day. He became extraordinarily beautiful. Dazzling light and brightness overwhelmed the disciples. Peter, James and John saw a glimpse of Jesus' heavenly existence. I wonder why Jesus gave to them that special glorious view on his way to the cross?

Jesus' effort seems to be a wasted effort. In the coming days, John and James would seek their own kingdom glory, requesting to sit at Jesus' left and right hand in his reign. Peter would continue to push back against Jesus' commitment to the cross. And, of course, there are Peter's infamous denials of Jesus at his trial. Did it do any good for these to see Jesus in his glory?

If you're paying attention, every experience with God makes a difference in your life. After Peter saw the resurrected Christ, he likely looked back and added the transfiguration to his faith walk. Perhaps he was able to more faithfully stand against the persecution he face. Likewise, John could write with more certainty the visions of *Revelation* and the truth of the Gospel. As James died a martyr in the early church, would he have faced death with more certainty?

I don't know how this glorious display of the power of the kingdom of God affected these three. I do pray that you pay attention to Jesus' glory in your life—his saving death and resurrection, his love, and all the glory he offers to you, especially the glory of his salvation.

Pause and consider joyfully the glory of the Lord Jesus is for you.

A Good Place to Be

How Did They Know?

> *Mark 9:4-5 And there appeared before them Elijah and Moses, who were talking with Jesus. 5 Peter said to Jesus, "Rabbi, it is good for us to be here. Let us put up three shelters — one for you, one for Moses and one for Elijah."*

YOU likely have questions about biblical events. For example, in this passage, you might say, "How did the disciples know it was Moses and Elijah with Jesus? There weren't any pictures of them."

That's a good question, so here's a good answer. The disciples knew Moses' and Elijah's identity in the same way they knew God's words and purpose for their lives. The Spirit of God came in power to these prophets to inspire (cause them to know) them to inerrantly (without error) proclaim and write the truth of God.

The Spirit of God moved over the disciples that day to reveal Moses' and Elijah's identity. God, the Father, desired to make a specific point to James, John and Peter. He needed them to know some things. And he used Elijah and Moses to show them.

Perhaps what he wanted to show them was Jesus' glory contrasted to these great prophets. Jesus had come to complete the Law of Moses. And there are many comparisons with Elijah's and Jesus' ministry—Elijah's survival in a wilderness, an unending supply of food for a widow, and Elijah's resurrection of her son.

Moses and Elijah were grand and glorious prophets of the LORD, but they were not and are not the Son of God. God, the Father, has to make it clear to James, Peter and John that Jesus is more than a prophet. And so he does.

Pause and consider that none can compare to the Christ.

Find Jesus Follow Jesus

Jesus Transfigures You

> Mark 9:6-8 (He did not know what to say, they were so frightened.) 7 Then a cloud appeared and enveloped them, and a voice came from the cloud: "This is my Son, whom I love. Listen to him!" 8 Suddenly, when they looked around, they no longer saw anyone with them except Jesus.

YOU'VE been there. Something wonderful and marvelous happens—perhaps it was your wedding day; perhaps it was the birth of your children; perhaps it was the moment you recognized Jesus as your Lord. In the moment, you were overwhelmed with joy as you felt God's hand on you.

James, John and Peter are watching Jesus taking on great beauty right before their eyes. Peter is speechless. He is experiencing, for an instant, what his heavenly future will look like. Heaven's glory and beauty from a human point of view is a frightening experience.

The Bible repeatedly shows to you that the people who experience God's glory on earth become frightened at the approach of a heavenly being. God's purity is so great, our sinful hearts and minds cannot easily deal with him. Fear grips you when you realize you are in the hands of the sovereign God whose wrath against sin demands his perfect judgment on your life. It is only in this kind of fear that you will awaken to the truth that, (Romans 3:23) *for all have sinned and fall short of the glory of God.*

When you realize that awful truth, I pray you will see the heavenly beauty of this glorious truth that (Romans 5:8) *But God demonstrates his own love for us in this: While we were still sinners, Christ died for us.*

Turn your fear to faith. Receive heaven's glory that transfigures you and makes *you* beautiful before God.

Pause and consider God transfigures you from sin into life eternal.

A Good Place to Be

Sounds Foolish

> *Mark 9:9-10 As they were coming down the mountain, Jesus gave them orders not to tell anyone what they had seen until the Son of Man had risen from the dead. 10 They kept the matter to themselves, discussing what "rising from the dead" meant.*

WHAT IF you went to a church, and the pastor told you that he must die to do God's will? And then he would rise from the dead on the 3rd day after his death. What would you say?

You'd probably be as the disciples were—confused! "What does Jesus mean about 'rising from the dead—coming out of the grave? Certainly not! No one's ever done that. Maybe he means he'll leave and come back on the 3rd day. Or maybe he's going to go into seclusion for 3 days, and it will seem to be death. Jesus isn't making any sense.'"

No, Jesus' language of dying and rising again made absolutely no sense to the disciples. And the truth is, the Apostle Paul writes that it is even foolishness to the unbeliever:

(1 Corinthians 1:18-19) *For the message of the cross is foolishness to those who are perishing, but to us who are being saved it is the power of God. 19 For it is written: "I will destroy the wisdom of the wise; the intelligence of the intelligent I will frustrate."*

Do you see how it is some will not believe? They will consider Jesus' words and the testimony of the Apostles to Christ's resurrection as foolishness.

So please, don't be ashamed to tell the "foolish" story. Some will believe. Some won't. Let God decide who does and doesn't. After all, it's God's story.

Pause and consider the unbelievable wonder of God's grace to save you—and rejoice!

Will Elijah Come Again?

> Mark 9:11 And they asked him, "Why do the teachers of the law say that Elijah must come first?"

ARE YOU confused? After all, the disciples are talking about Elijah, the prophet, 800 years gone from earth. And they're asking Jesus about the teachers who say, "Elijah must come first and restore all things." Who and what are they talking about?

Here's who and what: Elijah was a prophet who lived around 850 BC. He lived in caves and was a pretty rough character—he needed a shave and some new clothes. God used him to speak significant judgment against Israel's kings, and then God did this: In *2 Kings 2:11 As Elijah and Elisha were walking along and talking together, suddenly a chariot of fire and horses of fire appeared and separated the two of them, and Elijah went up to heaven in a whirlwind.*

He went right to Heaven! Then about 400 years before Christ comes Malachi, the prophet, says this: (*Malachi 4:5-6*) *"See, I will send you the prophet Elijah before that great and dreadful day of the Lord comes. 6 He will turn the hearts of the fathers to their children, and the hearts of the children to their fathers; or else I will come and strike the land with a curse."*

The Jews expect Elijah's return to bring healing and judgment to them. And it will come before the "day of the Lord"—the judgment of the Messiah. Having just seen Elijah at the transfiguration, the disciples are trying to confirm Malachi's prophesy and ask, "Does Elijah need to come first?"

You'll see Jesus' answer on the next page. The lesson to learn here is this: To know the true meaning of God's Word, you must go to God's word to uncover its grand meaning for your life now and forever.

Pause and consider how necessary God's Word is to know.

A Good Place to Be

Elijah Has Come

> Mark 9:12-13 Jesus replied, "To be sure, Elijah does come first, and restores all things. Why then is it written that the Son of Man must suffer much and be rejected? 13 But I tell you, Elijah has come, and they have done to him everything they wished, just as it is written about him."

YOU remember the question from the previous page? Must Elijah, the prophet from about 850 BC, come back to life before the Messiah would come as Malachi prophesied? The disciples are sure Jesus is the Messiah. Where's Elijah?

As Jesus replies, "*To be sure, Elijah does come first, and restores all things.*" Jesus is affirming the doctrine of Malachi's prophecy that a prophet would appear just before the Messiah to "restore" the Jews understanding of the Messiah's appearance and work in the world. This prophet would reform the people to an attitude of repentance and greater consideration of their sin and God's judgment. The one who did that was John the Baptist. He's the "Elijah".

Before the coming of John the Baptist, the understanding of the day was that the Messiah would rule with conquering authority. They had forgotten or left out the prophecies of his suffering and death. When Jesus asked, "*Why then is it written that the Son of Man must suffer much and be rejected?*" he is reminding his disciples of the Scriptures' truth. In essence, Jesus says, "Yes, one as Elijah—John the Baptist—has come. And as long as I'm teaching you about that prophecy, let me remind you about me—I must suffer and die. Remember that."

The Jews, the disciples and you need the full picture of the Messiah. Are you missing anything?

Pause and consider how vital it is to know all about Jesus.

Find Jesus Follow Jesus

Jesus the Protector

> Mark 9:14-16 When they came to the other disciples, they saw a large crowd around them and the teachers of the law arguing with them. 15 As soon as all the people saw Jesus, they were overwhelmed with wonder and ran to greet him. 16 "What are you arguing with them about?" he asked.

JESUS IS a good rabbi. You might say, "That's obvious. He should be a good rabbi. He's perfect in knowledge." You're right. But I want to "show" you a less obvious way he's a good rabbi. Do you see him taking care of his disciples here?

Just back from his transfiguration on the mountaintop, Jesus is likely feeling the power of the Spirit on him in a relaxed, refreshing way. I think one of the reasons he went to the mountaintop was to be invigorated with the personal presence of the Father and the Spirit. Refreshed, Jesus is ready for action. Then action comes.

Many in the crowd with his disciples waiting run up to meet him. They longed to see him. His disciples were glad to see him, too. They needed him. The teachers of the law were arguing with them. Do you see that Jesus walks past the people excitedly crowding around him to take care of his disciples? Jesus knows the teachers are trying to turn the crowd against the disciples and possibly turn the disciples against Jesus. Jesus has left them, and through these teachers, Satan is attacking his main leadership team.

Asking, "What are you arguing about?" he breaks in and begins to take control. Jesus is a good rabbi. He's a great leader. He cares for and protects his own.

Pause and consider how you are to protect your family and friends against Satan's attacks.

A Good Place to Be

Can't You Do It?

> *Mark 9:17-19 A man in the crowd answered, "Teacher, I brought you my son, who is possessed by a spirit that has robbed him of speech. 18 Whenever it seizes him, it throws him to the ground. He foams at the mouth, gnashes his teeth and becomes rigid. I asked your disciples to drive out the spirit, but they could not." 19 "O unbelieving generation," Jesus replied, "how long shall I stay with you? How long shall I put up with you? Bring the boy to me."*

JESUS approaches his disciples arguing with the teachers. What's the argument? It seems to be over the disciples' inability to heal the demon-possessed boy. The teachers are likely discrediting the disciples and Jesus because they have no ability to heal in Jesus' name. With their Lord gone to the mountaintop, they seem to lose faith in their Lord.

A similar faith lesson is found in Moses' ascent to the mountain to get the Ten Commandments. When he returned, he found his people, led by his brother Aaron, had made a golden calf idol to worship. When the prophet was gone, the people lost their faith in God.

That's why Jesus is upset. He's upset at the teachers of the law who knew of Moses and many other times the Jews had lost their faith in God. And he's upset his disciples have too little faith to do the work he has taught them to do. Their work is a faith work. They must be faith-filled to do the work.

Once again, the Lord comes to do what no one else can do. He is dismayed knowing someday he will be gone. His desire is to leave the world in faithful hands.

Pause and consider: are you Jesus' faithful hands today?

| Find Jesus Follow Jesus

The King Takes Control

Mark 9:20-22 So they brought him. When the spirit saw Jesus, it immediately threw the boy into a convulsion. He fell to the ground and rolled around, foaming at the mouth. 21 Jesus asked the boy's father, "How long has he been like this?" "From childhood," he answered.

IS JESUS around your life? I know he wants to be, but is he? Do you let his authority rule your thoughts, your desires, your actions, and your relationships?

How does that kind of life happen? You can look to the disciples to see how Jesus' authority ruled their lives. As young men, they had little purpose.

But when Jesus showed up to say, "Follow me." their lives began to come under his authority. Step-by-step they grew in their understanding of Jesus' teachings, his love, his forgiveness and his healing. Mark 9 shows you they had many steps to go to fully know Jesus' authority in all things. They couldn't do a heeling Jesus expected them to do. He had to take control of the scene. But scripture shows us they would eventually learn (read *Acts*).

Under Jesus' authority the disciples' lives became purposeful world-changing lives. Their thoughts, desires, actions and relationships were totally based on their faith in Jesus Christ. They lived as few human beings ever have lived as Jesus anointed them with his Spirit in power and in truth.

What about you? What do you think God *really* wants you to do? Are you afraid to really ask? The task might be too crazy, too "out there". But who knows, maybe you'll get to change the world around you.

To find out, center your life on Jesus' authority.

Pause and consider Jesus' authority brings order and purpose to your life.

A Good Place to Be

A Good Prayer

> Mark 9:23-25 "'If you can'?" said Jesus. "Everything is possible for him who believes." 24 Immediately the boy's father exclaimed, "I do believe; help me overcome my unbelief!" 25 When Jesus saw that a crowd was running to the scene, he rebuked the evil spirit. "You deaf and mute spirit," he said, "I command you, come out of him and never enter him again."

YOU and I are like the boy's father, aren't we? We try to believe in all Jesus has for us—his unending love, his forgiveness and his healing to name a few. Especially in times of distress we wonder, "Will Jesus care for me in my need? Where is he for my sick mom, my lost daughter, my broken heart? Do I have the faith he requires of me?

Answering that faith question can challenge you. You have to look into our heart and ask, "What do I believe about Jesus?" You must examine our own lives to determine, "Do I trust the power the Gospel writers so readily demonstrate? Do I have the faith to believe "Everything is possible for him who believes"?

To get to that kind of faith, you must engage in a process of filling your mind with God's Word, filling your heart with God's love and praying the prayer the father prayed, "I do believe; help me overcome my unbelief!"

Believe in Jesus to believe he will answer that prayer and grow your faith. He truly wants you to know "Everything is possible for him who believes." Jesus often scolds his disciples for their lack of faith. But they grew in faith to do the work he needed them to do.

So can you.

Pause and consider that growing faith requires growing commitment to your Lord.

Find Jesus Follow Jesus

Strong Hold

> Mark 9:26 The spirit shrieked, convulsed him violently and came out. The boy looked so much like a corpse that many said, "He's dead." 27 But Jesus took him by the hand and lifted him to his feet, and he stood up.

THIS IS a scary scripture. If you don't think sin is a serious problem in your life, think again. Sin desires a death grip on you. Sin sneaks in and grabs hold. Only the Holy God has the power to break its deadly grip.

I saw a news spot on television tonight about a man in a homeless shelter. Alcohol and gambling addictions have broken his life. He lost his wife, his family, his home, and even the barest essentials of a physical existence. Sin's addictive grip had such a hold on him that it nearly killed him until the power of God rescued him.

It's easy to judge him and say, "Why didn't you stop?" But how does sin grip you? I look around, and I easily see so many "addictions" in people's lives. It grieves me to see people refusing care because prideful sin firmly blocks their humility. I see couples unwilling to stop their sinful "me-first" hearts, refusing to *"submit to one another out of reverence for Christ"* (Eph 5:21). I see my own heart sometimes with the sin of "too busy' to stop and *"be still and know I am God"* (Psalms 46:10).

Yes, sinful habits grab you, hold you and cause you to be deaf to hearing the word of God and mute to praising God. Jesus' power is the only sin-conquering power.

Pause and consider Jesus strength is for your freedom.

A Good Place to Be

Why Pray?

> *Mark 9:28-29 After Jesus had gone indoors, his disciples asked him privately, and "Why couldn't we drive it out?" 29 He replied, "This kind can come out only by prayer."*

YOU may ask, "Why pray if God already knows what's happening?" Answer: He wants your faith. God desires you to be engaged in faithfully seeking his power to guide your life.

This entire incident we've viewed over the past few pages is all about faith. Jesus sees that his disciples can't drive out the demon. He challenges the boy's father to a believing faith, and he shows these witnesses that he, the Lord and Savior, will respond if faithfully asked.

"If I can?" Jesus asked the doubting father. "O unbelieving generation." Jesus chastises his disciples. Yes, Jesus wants you to pray in faith that he will heal you, that he will change you, and that he will bring to you the will of God the Father.

Sometimes we parents do this with our children. You wait for them to ask for a ride to the store, a special treat, or a game of catch. You're often willing to do what they desire. You often know what they desire. Yet you wait, because you want them to faithfully feel they can come to you. You want them to trust you, don't you? Of course you do. You're a good parent, and trust is a big part of a loving, close relationship.

That's who your God is. He made you in his image. Your care for your child reflects his care for you. He wants you to faithfully ask him your desires and your needs, so you can grow into a faithful, loving friendship with him.

Pause and consider prayer will grow your love relationship with Jesus.

Find Jesus Follow Jesus

Private Talk

> Mark 9:30-32 *They left that place and passed through Galilee. Jesus did not want anyone to know where they were, 31 because he was teaching his disciples. He said to them, "The Son of Man is going to be betrayed into the hands of men. They will kill him, and after three days he will rise." 32 But they did not understand what he meant and were afraid to ask him about it.*

HAVE you ever been in a circumstance where you *had to learn* something really important, and you had little time to do so? Cramming for the test or memorizing your part for the Christmas play, there are thousands of reasons to know and remember knowledge that can make a big difference in your life temporarily or for a very long time.

Jesus teaches the disciples "need to know now" truth, but *"they did not understand what he meant and were afraid to ask him about it."* Why not? Could it be the same reason you don't understand the teaching from the Lord? Is the Bible so clear that you refuse its truth?

The disciples didn't like what they heard. They were afraid to pursue the truth because Jesus' words forced them to see their lives differently. They didn't see that Jesus must die, so they could live eternally. Too focused on their own understanding, their minds and hearts refused to listen. They couldn't adjust to Jesus' "right now" teaching.

Is your life that way? Do you "hear" God's word as you read the Bible; yet, you neither believe nor understand? Do you hide behind ignorance in fear because accepting God's word would mean dramatic change for you?

Pause and consider the truth is information you need to know right now.

A Good Place to Be

First in Line

> *Mark 9:33-35 They came to Capernaum. When he was in the house, he asked them, "What were you arguing about on the road?" 34 But they kept quiet because on the way they had argued about who was the greatest. 35 Sitting down, Jesus called the Twelve and said, "If anyone wants to be first, he must be the very last, and the servant of all."*

DON'T YOU just hate it when your kids argue over who's first? There's such a "me" attitude in that argument, isn't there? You wonder, "Why can't they just let each other 'go first' without a hassle?"

Are you willing to let others "go first"? You want things when you want them, and if someone tells you, "Wait." or "No, you must consider others' needs, opinions or point-of-view also." You get impatient, sometimes angry, and you say, "Me first!"

That's your sinful pride pushing you to be first in line in your own mind. You just know that your desires and ways are more important than anyone else's. After all, you have a right to be happy, to have all you want, to get what you long for, don't you?

Not according to Jesus. Your first purpose in living a right life in the Kingdom of God is to serve. You are to serve to others' needs with a humble and loving heart: (1 John 4:20(b) *anyone who does not love his brother, whom he has seen, cannot love God, whom he has not seen."* John warns you that a loving attitude to *everyone* is essential for your right relationship with God. When you love, you eagerly serve. When you serve, you are pleasing God.

Pause and consider that pleasing God puts you "first" in line at the King's throne.

Find Jesus Follow Jesus

Welcome the Son

> Mark 9:36-37 He took a little child and had him stand among them. Taking him in his arms, he said to them, 37 "Whoever welcomes one of these little children in my name welcomes me; and whoever welcomes me does not welcome me but the one who sent me."

THIS scripture is often used to point you to the truth that Jesus welcomed children—he loved and honored them. As he takes the child in his arms, you see the expression of a loving Savior who honors a child with his touch and his affirming words.

But look at something else. Do you see how Jesus equates honoring the child with honoring him? When you honor the child, you honor the one who loves the child—Jesus.

Then see how Jesus equates honoring him with honoring God, the Father. When you honor Jesus, you are honoring the Father.

How does this work in your family life? What about your home? Dads, when you honor your wife, you are honoring others who love her—her parents, her children and her siblings. Wives, when you honor your husband, you are honoring your children, his parents and his siblings. And children, when you honor your parents, you are also honoring your siblings and your grandparents.

Honor to one, whether it is the Son of God or the son of your parents, is an expression of love to those who love him. You are connected emotionally to many people. Wouldn't it be good, wouldn't it be godly to have that connection be love?

Pause and consider that love is the connection Jesus commanded.

A Good Place to Be

"Not One of Us"

> Mark 9:38-40 "Teacher," said John, "we saw a man driving out demons in your name and we told him to stop, because he was not one of us." 39 "Do not stop him," Jesus said. "No one who does a miracle in my name can in the next moment say anything bad about me, 40 for whoever is not against us is for us.

DO YOU think John learns slowly, if at all? In a series of teachings, Jesus has told his disciples, "The last shall be first." Then, "Let the little children come to me." And Jesus has shown the power of faithful prayer to heal.

Then John and the others report how they have tried to stop a man who was driving out demons. "He's not one of us, Jesus." Let's see, John, the man is faithfully healing in Jesus' name. How can he not be "one of us"?

Jesus' reply encourages his disciples to give the faithful healer leeway. Yes, they could have been concerned about his beliefs and why he was doing what he was doing. But Jesus points out that this man cannot oppose him as he heals in Jesus' name. Jesus has been calling his disciples to the kind of faith the man has. He tells them to celebrate the man's work because he is demonstrating Kingdom truth. As he does so, he is "one of us".

Be cautious of criticizing other ministries. They may not look the same as the church you're used to attending, but God empowers faithful people in many, many ways to do his will on earth. Look to other Christians as "one of us". And rejoice in their work. God uses different ministries for different purposes. Celebrate how he uses you.

Pause and consider the power God's people being united for him.

Find Jesus Follow Jesus

Be Kind to Jesus' Own

> Mark 9:41 *I tell you the truth, anyone who gives you a cup of water in my name because you belong to Christ will certainly not lose his reward.*

JESUS has been teaching his disciples about being humble and faithfully ministering to a world in need of Him. Then he gives them these encouraging words. In essence he is saying, "I will honor those who honor you. As you are my disciples, you belong to me. People who honor you honor me." This is an example of how your kind acts of love to one person will honor those whom that person loves and those who love him.

Think of how intimate and wonderful is your relationship with Jesus, the Lord of Creation, Savior and Friend! As you confess Jesus as your Savior and follow his teachings, you lovingly belong to him. Jesus "owns" you as a loving and honored possession. You are so highly valuable to him; he will never let you go. Taking it even more personally, you are a member of his body. You honor and care for your body, don't you? Jesus cares for you.

However, sometimes parts of your body are challenged with injury or illness, and that part needs care. Jesus knows, as he tells his disciples many times, that following him may cause you, a part of his body, to experience physical deprivation—hunger, thirst, injury. When that happens, you will be glad for a cup of cold water. Jesus will reward those who come to care for you because they are honoring you, one who Jesus loves, and they are honoring Jesus.

Do you know a Jesus follower who needs some special kindness today? Care for Jesus' own. Honor Jesus' own. Honor Jesus.

Pause and consider how kind Jesus is to save you. Be kind to his own.

A Good Place to Be

Harming Your Children?

> Mark 9:42-45 "And if anyone causes one of these little ones who believe in me to sin, it would be better for him to be thrown into the sea with a large millstone tied around his neck. 43 If your hand causes you to sin, cut it off. It is better for you to enter life maimed than with two hands to go into hell, where the fire never goes out. 45 And if your foot causes you to sin, cut it off. It is better for you to enter life crippled than to have two feet and be thrown into hell.

JESUS proclaims how deadly is the sin to destroy others by causing them to sin. A destroyer's destination is sure. It is hell and death.

Now I know you didn't want to hear that. You want to hear Jesus is all-loving and all-compassionate. Well, he is. He has such love and compassion for his creation that he will destroy people who harm those who seek him.

The millstone "necklace" is a deadly image. A millstone was a very large heavy stone used to crush grain. Jesus was the best at creating the perfect illustration for his teachings. And this millstone illustration is his teaching: Do not harm my own at the penalty of certain death.

Now parents, please stop and think. Is there any way you're harming your children's relationship with Jesus? Are you continually living an immoral life? Are you letting your children skip Bible class for sports? Are you neglecting God's Word in your home? Are you modeling "skipping church"? What is your home's priority—destroying God's Word or building on God's Word?

Pause and consider the harm you do neglecting God's Word.

Find Jesus Follow Jesus

Keep A Jesus Focus

> Mark 9:47-48 *And if your eye causes you to sin, pluck it out. It is better for you to enter the kingdom of God with one eye than to have two eyes and be thrown into Hell, 48 where "their worm does not die, and the fire is not quenched."*

THE Hymn says, "Turn your eyes upon Jesus. Look full in his wonderful face. And the things of earth will grow strangely dim in the light of his glory and grace." The song is an offering to your mind and soul to keep a Jesus focus in your life. It is his glory that must guide and guard you.

I hope Jesus' scary words here frighten and stir you to action regarding the focus of your own life and the lives of your loved ones. I pray you are urgent to tell them to turn their eyes upon Jesus whether they like to hear it or not.

Yes, they need to know they must focus their full attention on Jesus. One eye on Jesus and one eye on the world is no eye on Jesus. You get double vision. You think you see Jesus, but the world confuses your view. You don't know what direction is the right direction. When you don't know the right direction, you become lost, and "lost" is a word Jesus uses for people who have no eye on him.

You don't want to be lost. The lost go to Hell, *where "their worm does not die, and the fire is not quenched."* Consider the horror. Turn your eyes to Jesus, the way to Heaven.

Pause and consider how joyful are those who fully see Jesus.

A Good Place to Be

Hot Salt/Forever Salt

> Mark 9:49-50 *Everyone will be salted with fire. 50 "Salt is good, but if it loses its saltiness, how can you make it salty again? Have salt in yourselves, and be at peace with each other."*

HOW would you feel being "salted with fire"? Someone is shaking a big salt shaker over you, and hot fiery salt pours out all over your body. Awful image, isn't it? Yes, that is the image of eternal torment.

Then Jesus offers a second salt image. Salt is a way of life. The "life salt" comes when you have salt in you. What does that mean? To answer that question, you can go to Jesus' teaching in Matthew 5:13 *"You are the salt of the earth. But if the salt loses its saltiness, how can it be made salty again? It is no longer good for anything, except to be thrown out and trampled by men."*

Salt was vital to that culture to preserve food. Food was life. Bad salt did no preserving. If one put bad salt on food to preserve it, the food spoiled. Bad salt meant death. Good salt meant life.

You have the "good salt" life from your Lord: (Matthew 19:17) *"If you want to enter life, obey the commandments."* Obeying Jesus, you have salt in you. Then you are the one who offers to the world the life-preserving truth of Jesus Christ. Put his commands on your heart. Put his salt in you and live. And spread the salt to others.

Pause and consider Jesus' truth preserves your life.

Find Jesus Follow Jesus

Precious Gift

> Mark 10:1-9 *Jesus then left that place and went into the region of Judea and across the Jordan. Again crowds of people came to him, and as was his custom, he taught them. 2 Some Pharisees came and tested him by asking, "Is it lawful for a man to divorce his wife?" 3 "What did Moses command you?" he replied. 4 They said, "Moses permitted a man to write a certificate of divorce and send her away." 5 "It was because your hearts were hard that Moses wrote you this law," Jesus replied. 6 "But at the beginning of creation God 'made them male and female.' 7 'For this reason a man will leave his father and mother and be united to his wife, 8 and the two will become one flesh.' So they are no longer two, but one. 9 Therefore what God has joined together, let man not separate."*

YOU often want to see if there is "another way", don't you? What I mean is the constant assessment of each thing you do with the question, "Does this really apply to me?" You wonder if you can fudge on the doctor's order to reduce your food intake. You question the need to hold your children accountable. You prefer to make the choices regarding your faith. "I'll believe what fits me."

As the Pharisees ask the divorce question, Jesus gives the reason Moses allowed it. The people of Moses' day and throughout history have put marriage into a convenience place. "Does God really want us to be married forever?" People look for ways out of marriage instead of ways to stay in it.

When Jesus says, "*Therefore what God has joined together, let man not separate.*" he proclaims God's truth and purpose for marriage. Marriage is precious, and you must work to keep it safe.

Pause and consider God's true word is his loving gift to you. Cherish all he says.

A Good Place to Be

Speak of Jesus

> Mark 10:10 *When they were in the house again, the disciples asked Jesus about (divorce). 11 He answered, "Anyone who divorces his wife and marries another woman commits adultery against her. 12 And if she divorces her husband and marries another man, she commits adultery."*

DO YOU think Jesus is realistic here? After all, many marriages end in divorce. Surely this is the thing to do when we can't get along isn't it? Why would Jesus call a second marriage adultery?

This "divorce discourse" in today's and yesterday's scriptures is a focus on God's intended purpose in marriage. He created marriage to be a lifelong bond of a one-flesh relationship through God that (Matt 19:6) "*man (shall) not separate*"

But then sin divided or "divorced" that relationship. Divorce came into the world just as murder, theft and idolatry came as people turned from God. They took their eyes from the Lord and fixed their eyes on themselves and their own desires. Thus, when we see this black and white command, we think, "What does it really mean? Divorced people aren't married. They're free to marry again."

Jesus' commands are aimed at people who casually divorce without cause. Too many people initiate divorce to satisfy sensual pleasures. This is sin, and this kind of divorce is sin that leads to more sin.

A sin-influenced mind has brought great destruction on marriages. Strive as you can to stay true to God. Protect your marriage. Read God's Word together. Pray for each other. When you do these things, you will desire God's ways for your marriage. Ask the Holy Spirit to focus you on Jesus. Stay strong against sin. Stay married. If sin has stolen your spouse, pray for their repentance and know God wants to ease the ache in your heart.

Pause and consider how focusing on God will keep your marriage good.

Find Jesus Follow Jesus

A Blessed Touch

> Mark 10:13-16 *People were bringing little children to Jesus to have him touch them, but the disciples rebuked them. 14 When Jesus saw this, he was indignant. He said to them, "Let the little children come to me, and do not hinder them, for the kingdom of God belongs to such as these. 15 I tell you the truth; anyone who will not receive the kingdom of God like a little child will never enter it." 16 And he took the children in his arms, put his hands on them and blessed them.*

OUR culture has become a very "non-touch" culture. Part of it is based on a northern European heritage. Part of it is based on a great fear of inappropriate touch. And part of it is just plain ignorance of the power of a loving touch. Psychological, spiritual, medical and relational studies have repeatedly demonstrated that a loving touch from one person to another is an honoring, life-giving gesture.

In a recent class at our church on John Trent's book "The Blessing", a group discovered that the Bible always records that Jesus touched those he healed. The Bible shows the power *and the necessity* of the loving touch as a means to pass forward a blessing—an honor, a validation—from one generation to the next.

People didn't just want him to speak to their children, they wanted Jesus to *touch* them! When the disciples said, "No." he turned and said to them, "No." Then he *gathered them in his arms*.

How beautiful is this picture of a loving creator, honoring his creation. He's showing you parents, grandparents, mentors, honored friends what you need to do—bless the children with loving touch.

Pause and consider how Jesus' reaches from the cross to bless you.

A Good Place to Be

Jesus Isn't Good?

> Mark 10:17-18 *As Jesus started on his way, a man ran up to him and fell on his knees before him. "Good teacher," he asked, "what must I do to inherit eternal life?" 18 "Why do you call me good?" Jesus answered. "No one is good — except God alone."*

DO YOU have the heart of this young man that caused him to *run* up to Jesus and fall at his knees before him? That's a good kind of heart to have—a heart eagerly seeking Heaven's eternal truths to know *"what must I do to inherit eternal life".*

When you have a question that needs a best answer, what do you do? Do you, as this man did, find the best authority available to you? I hope so. That's what this man was doing—seeking the truth of Heaven from the One who was demonstrating Heaven's Truth come to earth.

When Jesus replies to the man's greeting, "Good teacher" by saying, *"No one is good—except God alone."* he wants the man to recognize him as God. Before he teaches the man the truths of Heaven, Jesus wants the man to know he is talking not to a good teacher, but he is talking to the true God.

Goodness is of God. Goodness comes only from God. Only God is good, and when you call Jesus "good" know he is not simply a teacher who teaches "good" things, but know he is God who teaches God's truths.

The man came running to the Truth to find the truth of Heaven. He dropped to his knees humbly willing to hear the truth. He did not come casually. He came passionately desiring answers. Is that what you do when you come to church?

Pause and consider: how passionately do you seek the truth?

Find Jesus Follow Jesus

Jesus Loved Him

> Mark 10:19-21 *"You know the commandments: 'Do not murder, do not commit adultery, do not steal, do not give false testimony, do not defraud, honor your father and mother.'" 20 "Teacher," he declared, "all these I have kept since I was a boy." 21 Jesus looked at him and loved him.*

WHY DO you think God gave to you the Ten Commandments? Do you think it was to restrict you or free you? Do you think it was to dominate you or to love you?

When the young man asked Jesu*s, "What must I do to inherit eternal life?"* (Mark 10:17), Jesus responded with 6 of the Ten Commandments to point the man to God's Law. Jesus' reference to 6 commandments in no way restricts the rest of the Law. He was simply illustrating the source of Truth and the means to inherit eternal life began with the Law.

Then Jesus looks on him and loves him. God giving the Law to his people was a loving act of the God who is love. Love pours forth from God's Son to the young man as it had poured forth from the Father to Moses and as it pours forth from the Spirit onto you today.

See in the Holy Bible that his love pours out onto you, so that you know the answer to the question, "What must I do to inherit eternal life?" God's answer is clear: "I love you. Obey the commandments I lovingly gave you. Live in the grace and love I offer to you. Believe in me. Truly make me Lord of your life. Do this, and you will have eternal life."

Yes, Jesus loved the man with his answer. Jesus loves you. Listen to him.

Pause and consider how knowing the right way is God's love way.

A Good Place to Be

Why So Sad?

> Mark 10:21-23 Jesus looked at him and loved him. "One thing you lack," he said. "Go, sell everything you have and give to the poor, and you will have treasure in heaven. Then come, follow me." 22 At this the man's face fell. He went away sad, because he had great wealth. 23 Jesus looked around and said to his disciples, "How hard it is for the rich to enter the kingdom of God!"

JESUS answered the young man's question, "*What must I do to inherit eternal life?*" telling him of the commandments and clearly loving him. What more did the man want? Apparently he wanted his way.

That's the thing isn't it? You're willing to ask Jesus, "What must I do?" but are you willing to *do* what the Lord requires of you? Since the dawn of time, humanity has said to its creator, "Lord, I like *most* of what you said, but I can't quite do that 'one thing'. I can't keep my hands off the forbidden fruit. I can't go into that city to preach repentance. I can't go to worship you as you call me. I can't give up my self-purpose for your purpose. I can't offer my life to you. You can have *most* of my life, Lord, but you can't have it all."

If that sounds too familiar, then pause and consider that you really don't want to call Jesus "Lord". Failing to give him all of your life, he is not Lord of your life. You remain your own lord. God will not tolerate competition.

The young man went home worshiping his money more than Jesus. Do you think he inherited eternal life as he desired?

Pause and consider what it means to you to call Jesus, "Lord".

Find Jesus Follow Jesus

Why So Amazed?

> Mark 10:24-27 *The disciples were amazed at his words. But Jesus said again, "Children, how hard it is to enter the kingdom of God! 25 It is easier for a camel to go through the eye of a needle than for a rich man to enter the kingdom of God." 26 The disciples were even more amazed, and said to each other, "Who then can be saved?" 27 Jesus looked at them and said, "With man this is impossible, but not with God; all things are possible with God."*

JESUS had just told a rich young man "Give up *everything!*" Then you are qualified to follow me. This is an extraordinary call to faith. The disciples were shocked. They were amazed. Why? Were they suddenly wondering if they, too, qualified to follow Jesus? But then Jesus speaks of even greater obstacles to the Kingdom: *"It is easier for a camel to go through the eye of a needle than for a rich man to enter the kingdom of God."*

Many have said that Jesus is referring to a camel going through a small gate in the city wall called the "eye of the needle". Truth is, Jesus is referring to the eye of a real needle. Amazed, the disciples are wondering what to do! *"Who then can be saved?"* Desperately they wonder, "How is it possible to enter the Kingdom of Heaven?" Then came Jesus' assurance: *"all things are possible with God."*

That is the Kingdom Truth. Only in God's power will you enter God's Kingdom. God has done a "God-thing" to save you as you faithfully confess Jesus as Lord. Recognize that truth. Rejoice in that truth. Nothing is impossible with God.

Pause and consider what "impossible" thing are you dealing with? Give to the all-powerful God.

A Good Place to Be

Bragging of Complaining?

> Mark 10:28 Peter said to him, "We have left everything to follow you!"

PETER'S words seem to shout off the page. Jesus had told the rich young man to leave everything to follow him. Now Peter is reminding his Lord, "That's exactly what we did, Jesus. Aren't we good?"

Also you can hear Peter desperately calling to Jesus. Jesus had also just said it was as impossible to enter the Kingdom of God as it would be for a camel to go through the eye of a real needle! Oh no! Peter and Jesus' other disciples are in a faith quandary. "We left everything. Will this save us? Was it worth it to leave our businesses, our possessions, our families, our futures to follow you, Jesus? What's the point if it's impossible to enter into the Kingdom?"

Either way, the disciples' attitude is out of faith. If they have been obedient to Jesus, they must humbly honor him as the one who called them to "give up all" and follow him. They must be grateful and joyful that the Lord has called them to his Kingdom.

If they are wondering if it's worth it to follow Jesus, they must consider that they gave up much, but there wasn't one thing of any value compared to the Kingdom promise.

These are good lessons. Do you ever think, "Jesus, look at what I've done for you!" Or do you ever wonder, "Jesus, is my sacrifice to you *worth it*? I've given up so much. All the fun I used to have, all the things I used to have, all the …."

Is anything more valuable than truly following God? Gladly leave the temporary, and you will gain the eternal.

Pause and consider how you really have no choice.

Find Jesus Follow Jesus

The Answer

> Mark 10:29-31 And Jesus replied, "Let me assure you that no one has ever given up anything-home, brothers, sisters, mother, father, children, or property-for love of me and to tell others the Good News, 30 who won't be given back, a hundred times over, homes, brothers, sisters, mothers, children, and land-with persecutions! "All these will be his here on earth, and in the world to come he shall have eternal life. 31 But many people who seem to be important now will be the least important then; and many who are considered least here shall be greatest there."

THE ONLY thing that could make life for my wife and me better than it is would be to live close to our daughter and her family. Seeing them about 4 weeks a year is a difficult circumstance. That separation essentially exists because of God's call on our lives to live and minister where we do. On the other hand, God has given us an incredible family of "parents, brothers, sisters, daughters, sons, and grandchildren" with a family of about 300 as we live and work with our Lord here.

That's what Jesus is describing to his disciples. He has told them they must leave everything for him. And he now tells them they will be rewarded with much more than they have left. Ministering the Gospel, they will live among people whom they will love and support. Their reward will be great.

There is, though, that one reference to persecutions. People will come against you as you talk of Jesus. They might make fun of you, avoid you, or even kill you.

Even so, there is the ultimate reward of eternal life—ultimate joy forever. How good is *that*?

Pause and consider: Temporary ends. Forever doesn't.

A Good Place to Be

Jesus Leads

> Mark 10:32-34 *They were on their way up to Jerusalem, with Jesus leading the way, and the disciples were astonished, while those who followed were afraid. Again he took the Twelve aside and told them what was going to happen to him. 33 "We are going up to Jerusalem," he said, "and the Son of Man will be betrayed to the chief priests and teachers of the law. They will condemn him to death and will hand him over to the Gentiles, 34 who will mock him and spit on him, flog him and kill him. Three days later he will rise."*

DO YOU see the picture? Jesus is walking to Jerusalem. The disciples are right behind him. Then other followers are next. The disciples are amazed. The others are afraid. Why?

They know the danger Jesus is walking into as he approaches Jerusalem. They know his accusers want to be rid of him. They are afraid Jesus' enemies will harm him and possibly persecute them. Their religious and government rulers are very oppressive.

But Jesus isn't oppressed. He is the amazing Lord, the Everlasting God who has the power and the strength to face and defeat all opposition. He carefully tells his disciples what will happen. Then he keeps going to Jerusalem, fearless of death, focused on life.

Are you afraid? Take heart and step into your Savior's footsteps. His victory for you is sure. He leads the way to the truth. Follow him. Arrive at the truth. Live in the truth, and your fears will no longer oppress you.

The disciples and Jesus' other followers would see him killed. They would see him rise. Their fear would leave them forever. See your crucified, risen Savior. Your fears will be gone, too.

Pause and consider: Jesus' truth destroys your fears.

Find Jesus Follow Jesus

Rather Presumptuous?

> *Mark 10:35 Then James and John, the sons of Zebedee, came to him. "Teacher," they said, "we want you to do for us whatever we ask."*

HAVE YOU ever said to Jesus, "Lord, I want you to do whatever I ask." I'm not sure if their tone was demanding, prayerful or even submissive. Regardless, how do you think they could be so presumptuous to expect Jesus to do "whatever they asked"?

Could it be they actually believed what Jesus had said? Look in John 14:13-14 and see this: *"And I will do whatever you ask in my name, so that the Son may bring glory to the Father. 14 You may ask me for anything in my name, and I will do it."* So, shouldn't Jesus do what they ask him to do? He said he would. Or did he?

John and James failed in their prayer. What they were asking was of *their own will*. They didn't make their request in Jesus' name. In other words, they failed to pray to the Father in the name of Jesus to seek the Father's will. That approach will never get your desires in line with God's desires—your will in line with God's will.

Jesus could not have been pleased at his presumptuous disciples. Their only desire should have been to glorify their Lord through a life of obedience to his will and not a life of "give us what we want."

Again it's time for them to learn a lesson about submitting their lives to truly follow Jesus. James and John need a lesson to turn their will to Jesus' will. What about you?

Pause and consider your prayers: Your will or God's will be done?

A Good Place to Be

Glorious Request

> Mark 10:36-40 "What do you want me to do for you?" he asked. 37 They replied, "Let one of us sit at your right and the other at your left in your glory." 38 "You don't know what you are asking," Jesus said. "Can you drink the cup I drink or be baptized with the baptism I am baptized with?" 39 "We can," they answered. Jesus said to them, "You will drink the cup I drink and be baptized with the baptism I am baptized with, 40 but to sit at my right or left is not for me to grant. These places belong to those for whom they have been prepared."

FLASHBACK about 3 years before this scripture. Jesus walks up to James and John fishing with their dad, and he says, "Follow me." In the 3 years since then to this day in their lives, these two simple fishermen who had no plans "past the boats" now have plans to sit at the right and left hand of the Messiah's throne! Wow.

But wait. Always the Good Shepherd, Jesus seeks to protect his confused sheep. He knows his baptism of the cross is near. He knows if James and John are to be considered for the throne room, they must endure their own crosses. He also knows it's up to the Father to decide James' and John's glory seats.

You read here an intense, powerful dialogue as Jesus warns the men about the cost of glory. He wants them to know beyond a doubt that terrible days are ahead, and he strives to prepare them.

He's that way with you, too. Following Jesus requires letting go of the past and preparing for everything the future holds—the crosses and the glory.

Pause and consider the Good Shepherd lovingly warns you, completely sustains you, thoroughly empowers you.

Find Jesus Follow Jesus

Get in Line

> Mark 10:41-45 When the ten heard about this, they became indignant with James and John. 42 Jesus called them together and said, "You know that those who are regarded as rulers of the Gentiles lord it over them, and their high officials exercise authority over them. 43 Not so with you. Instead, whoever wants to become great among you must be your servant, 44 and whoever wants to be first must be slave of all. 45 For even the Son of Man did not come to be served, but to serve, and to give his life as a ransom for many."

TEN disciples are angry with James and John for requesting their glory seats next to Jesus (see *Mark 10:36-40*). (Matthew 20:20 records their mother made the request—nice work, "mom".) The disciples are divided. "Division" is not a good word for people who live under the discipline of the Lord. (Note "disciple" in the root of discipline.) Now Jesus brings discipline to his disciples with the truth of his servant life.

You see, the disciples are worried about who will sit next to Jesus on an earthly throne. Jesus pointedly tells them that leadership in the Kingdom of God begins with servant hood to the point of death. Even more dramatically, he uses himself as the model of this life-sacrificing servant discipleship.

Think of this! The beloved Rabbi says, "I came to seek the lost. I came to save the lost. I came to die for you. Why are you fighting? Stop fighting among yourselves and start serving those who need my salvation!"

That's a good lesson for the church, and a good lesson for you.

Pause and consider: are you in line to be served or in line to serve?

A Good Place to Be

Son of David

> Mark 10:46-48 Then they came to Jericho. As Jesus and his disciples, together with a large crowd, were leaving the city, a blind man, Bartimaeus (that is, the Son of Timaeus), was sitting by the roadside begging. 47 When he heard that it was Jesus of Nazareth, he began to shout, "Jesus, Son of David, have mercy on me!" 48 Many rebuked him and told him to be quiet, but he shouted all the more, "Son of David, have mercy on me!"

JESUS continues his walk to Jerusalem. Picture a significant entourage of men and women who have supported the rabbi. They're anxious, hopeful and fearful. Jesus is fixed on his purpose.

Then comes the cry, *"Jesus, Son of David, have mercy on me!"* Who is this beggar who dares to interrupt the Rabbi? Why it is Bartimaeus, the blind beggar. He's *always* here along the road. But what does he say? He calls Jesus, "Son of David." Why would he say that?

He says it because it is true. The Jews know the Messiah will come from the family of David. Bartimaeus' cry is a profession of faith that the Messiah has come. Bartimaeus has heard the news of Jesus. Perhaps he has heard him teach. As Jesus walks by his begging place, Bartimaeus cries out to the Messiah.

Keep reading, and you'll see why. But for now take on this lesson. The blind man clearly sees the truth of Jesus. The Son of David has entered into his midst, and he will not let him depart without speaking his petition to him.

What do you need? Cry out to Jesus and let him know. It changed Bartimaeus. It will change you, too.

Pause and consider the cry of the faithful falls fully on Jesus' ears.

Find Jesus Follow Jesus

High Expectation

> Mark 10:49-50 Jesus stopped and said, "Call him." So they called to the blind man, "Cheer up! On your feet! He's calling you." 50 Throwing his cloak aside, he jumped to his feet and came to Jesus.

YOU'VE had a long day. Worse, it's been a long week. And even worse it's been a long, long time since you felt any joy or heard any hope in your heart as the Facebook friend who wrote, "I haven't smiled inside and out for a long time." Too often dark clouds seem to hover over your soul. You look around to see people enjoying life, loving others and being loved. You don't have the relationships you'd hoped for, or they have disappeared as loved ones are gone from your life. You wonder, "Why can't I have what they have?" You feel as an outcast. People talk to you, but no one knows what to really say because you seem so sad.

Then one day you hear a voice say, *"Jesus is here! Cheer up! On your feet! He's calling you."* What? Jesus is calling *me*? Why would he care about *me*? I'm a hopeless mess. I'm not loveable. Life is always handing me more heartache than I care to consider. Why would Jesus call me?

I'll tell you why Jesus calls to you. He loves you. I know you've heard that before, but listen! Get on your feet. Get out of your sad chair. Move off the couch of despair. Leave your sadness there and come see what the *Lord of Life has for you!*

Who knows, he might give you new eyes to see how wonderful life is when you let him take you by the hand.

Pause and consider the Savior beckons you—yes you.

A Good Place to Be

"I Want to See"

> Mark 10:51-52 *"What do you want me to do for you?" Jesus asked him. The blind man said, "Rabbi, I want to see." 52 "Go," said Jesus, "your faith has healed you." Immediately he received his sight and followed Jesus along the road.*

DO YOU notice Jesus asks Bartimaeus the same question he asked James and John (see Mark 10:36)? Whether a man was Jesus' close disciple or a blind beggar, Jesus brought the realm of all his power into play with that simple question.

How did Bartimaeus' answer differ from James' and John's answer, (Mark 10:37) *"Let one of us sit at your right and the other at your left in your glory."* Both answers are men honestly answering Jesus' question and expecting he'll do as asked.

But here's the difference. The disciples' answer was pointed at themselves. They expected Jesus to use his power and authority to glorify them; whereas, Bartimaeus' answer showed he trusted Jesus to use his power and authority over sin and sickness to glorify the Lord.

Bartimaeus didn't hold back saying, "I don't know. Could you possibly heal my eyes, Lord?" Or he didn't say, "Could I get a few coins for my next meal?" No, Bartimaeus didn't mince words. He was sick of his blindness. The one who could heal him had just asked him, "What do you want me to do for you?"

In the breath of the Spirit, that question comes from Jesus through God's Word upon you today. Jesus has made himself available to you. Get up and go to him in expectation. Then tell him what you passionately desire he does for you to bring glory to him today.

Pause and consider Jesus' power is the same transforming power as that day at Jericho.

Find Jesus Follow Jesus

Shout Hosanna

> Mark 11:7-10 *When they brought the colt to Jesus and threw their cloaks over it, he sat on it. 8 Many people spread their cloaks on the road, while others spread branches they had cut in the fields. 9 Those who went ahead and those who followed shouted, "Hosanna!" "Blessed is he who comes in the name of the Lord!" 10 "Blessed is the coming kingdom of our father David!" "Hosanna in the highest!"*

READING this, a praise song comes to me, "Shout to the Lord all the earth let us sing, power and majesty praise to the King." What a wonder it is to praise the name of Jesus.

When the day begins, praise the name of Jesus. When the noonday comes, praise the name of Jesus. When the night falls, praise the name of Jesus.

When you consider your troubles, praise the name of Jesus. When you are pleased in your blessings, praise the name of Jesus. When it's time to go to worship, praise the name of Jesus. When you come home from worship, praise the name of Jesus.

Jesus, the name above all names, the sweet name of loving restoration, the name of one who the Father sacrificed for you, the one who is risen, the one who sits at the right hand of the Father, the one who will come again, praise the name of Jesus.

Praise the name of the Beginning and the End. Praise the triumphant King. Praise the one who knocks at your door to come into your life. Praise the name of Jesus, who offers the forgiveness of sins.

Pause and consider the ways you praise Jesus.

| A Good Place to Be

Protect

> Mark 11:11 Jesus entered Jerusalem and went to the temple. He looked around at everything, but since it was already late, he went out to Bethany with the Twelve.

OFTEN the most profound messages come in the simplest phrases. Seeing our Lord walking to the Temple, looking around, and then leaving seems as if it's a scene out of reality TV where you are doing nothing watching someone else doing nothing. But something is happening here, and it's good for you to watch the Lord Jesus in action.

Yes, you might say, "He didn't do anything."

But he did. He is the Son of God, who made a "house check" his priority that day. As Jesus "looks around", he sees evidence of improper activities in the temple, his "house", and the temple is at risk. Jesus leaves and prepares to return the next day to do what he must to care for and cleanse his house.

Here's Jesus' lesson for you: Watch over your house. I'm not talking about the physical house. I'm talking about the "house" of relationships built on the foundational blocks of loving God and loving one another in the Lord's grace and truth. Your house is to be a loving, nourishing environment for all who enter and all who live there. Whatever blocks that from happening, you must get rid of it.

God built his temple to be a loving nourishing environment for his people. Jesus has come to "look around" the temple to know what he must do to protect the temple. On the next day he will act to clean his house from evil.

Keep your eyes open. Look around. What must you do to protect your house, to clean it of evil?

Pause and consider the threat is constant...constant... constant.

Find Jesus Follow Jesus

Frustrated Jesus

> *Mark 11:12-14 The next day as they were leaving Bethany, Jesus was hungry. 13 Seeing in the distance a fig tree in leaf, he went to find out if it had any fruit. When he reached it, he found nothing but leaves, because it was not the season for figs. 14 Then he said to the tree, "May no one ever eat fruit from you again." And his disciples heard him say it.*

HOW is your faith journey? Do you have a bigger faith than you did last year, last month or yesterday? Has anything changed in your life regarding what you believe Jesus can and will do? Or maybe your faith is growing, but you're moving *so slowly*. Hurry! There's so much good ahead for you. Jesus wants your faith life to be productive and fruitful.

When Jesus comes to the fig tree, he's wondering, "Where are the figs?" The phrase *"it was not the season for figs"* refers to the time to gather figs. Figs were actually present all year in Judea. And the truth about a fig tree is that it bears its fruit before it produces leaves.

Thus, when Jesus saw the leaves, he expected the fruit to be there. The "no fig" fig tree illustrates God's faithless, fruitless people.

For nearly 2,000 years God has been growing his people to the day of Jesus. But they do not know him as he walks into their lives. Rejecting and reshaping God's Word, they have no faith in God, and their lives are fruitless before God. Then Jesus gives you a picture of his coming judgment as he curses the fruitless tree.

Those whose faith is weak and without fruit will be condemned. Jesus has warned you.

Pause and consider: would Jesus find you fruitless?

A Good Place to Be

Jesus Loves His House

> Mark 11:15-17 On reaching Jerusalem, Jesus entered the temple area and began driving out those who were buying and selling there. He overturned the tables of the money changers and the benches of those selling doves, 16 and would not allow anyone to carry merchandise through the temple courts. 17 And as he taught them, he said, "Is it not written: "'My house will be called a house of prayer for all nations'? But you have made it 'a den of robbers.'"

JESUS is angry. This is the Judge, the Son of Man come to pass judgment on his people who do evil in his house.

Imagine if you go to your home, and you find people selling goods in your driveway, cattle in your entryway and people lending money in your kitchen. You'd be enraged wouldn't you? Your home was meant for family life, not business!

That's what is happening here. God, the Father, had caused this temple to be built as a holy place where his Word was taught and where people could go to find the safety and protection of the Father's mercy. God had built the temple in his image to display his pure love and care to his people.

But there are cattle and sheep in the outer courts. There is no room now to teach God's Word. Moneychangers replace the priests who should be offering sacrifices. God's law is ignored, neither taught nor obeyed. It's time for restoration of God's house.

As Jesus begins the cleansing, removing animals and moneychangers, Jesus is as a housekeeper sweeping the dirt out. He's removing the sin from the temple, so God's people would clearly see the Father.

Pause and consider how Jesus now cleans the dirt from you, his new temple.

| Find Jesus Follow Jesus

Don't Accuse Me!

> Mark 11:18 *The chief priests and the teachers of the law heard this and began looking for a way to kill him, for they feared him, because the whole crowd was amazed at his teaching.*

JESUS had just told the chief priests that they had made his temple *"a den of robbers"*. That's a serious charge, especially if he's right. Of course, Jesus is right. The chief priests who guide the temple and the worship there know he's right. They know the temple was built with God's glory as the focus. They know they have stolen away God's glory through their sinful acts.

What is the matter with them? Why do they resist Jesus' truth? Why do they plot to kill the truth? Why didn't they bow down and worship him?

I don't know. Are they, perhaps, afraid of the truth? Would they be acting in a way similar to you rejecting the truth of someone telling you, "You sin as you ignore God's Word. You have made God to be a liar because you don't trust his truth. You fail to pray, and you fail to love God. You waste time in worthless activities, running around seeking glory for yourself while you don't even consider you must act to glorify God."

What would you say if someone said that to you? Would you plot to "kill" them with negative comments, harsh words or rejection of their truth? Would you say to them, "Stop accusing me." even though you know they speak the truth?

The chief priests of the temple had acted to remove God from his own house. Have you acted to remove or keep God from your heart?

Pause and consider your actions and words. Are they about you or about God?

A Good Place to Be

Have Faith

> Mark 11:19-22 When evening came, they went out of the city. 20 In the morning, as they went along, they saw the fig tree withered from the roots. 21 Peter remembered and said to Jesus, "Rabbi, look! The fig tree you cursed has withered!" 22 "Have faith in God," Jesus answered.

JESUS had cursed the tree the day before because it did not bear fruit. Now that the tree is dead, he seems to be telling his disciples, "You could curse this tree, too, if you had faith in God."

But, instead, he's giving to them a life-giving warning. When he says, *"have faith in God"*, Jesus is reminding them that unbelief in God will cause their death. If they understand nothing else, they must know that without faith, they, just as the fruitless tree, will perish.

Jesus keeps pressing into his disciples to dramatically demonstrate his faith lessons for their lives. He has shown Peter, John and James his glory on the mountaintop. He has corrected John's and James' misconception of kingdom glory. He has demonstrated his glory in the blind Bartimaeus' healing. Jesus has cleansed his temple of sin. He has cursed a fruitless fig tree.

All of this is a picture of the future. People will enter into God's glory only as they believe Jesus' teaching. If they have no faith, they will die in the curse of blindness to the truth and sin in their unbelief. They will be condemned to Hell.

Jesus urgently says to his disciples, "Have faith in God." to clearly warn them of the penalty of a faithless life.

I urge you to consider your faith. Do you know Jesus is your Lord and Savior? Will your faith lead you to his glory?

Pause and carefully consider your answers.

Mountain Moving Prayer

> Mark 11:23-25 "I tell you the truth, if anyone says to this mountain, 'Go, throw yourself into the sea,' and does not doubt in his heart but believes that what he says will happen, it will be done for him. 24 Therefore I tell you, whatever you ask for in prayer, believe that you have received it, and it will be yours. 25 And when you stand praying, if you hold anything against anyone, forgive him, so that your Father in heaven may forgive you your sins."

YOU'RE likely wondering, "When has anyone prayed and a mountain moved into the sea? Surely there have been many people of great faith. Wouldn't someone have tried that prayer to prove Jesus correct? Maybe no one has. It would be such an amazing faith prayer: "Mountain, move!" But is that what Jesus is teaching here?

The mountain is symbolic in Jewish teachings. Mountains are the place of awesome power as God gave the law to them at Mt. Sinai. He also offered great demonstrations of power at Mt. Horeb. Mountains are also a place of protection. Jerusalem is on a mountain. Mountains symbolize God's holiness, power and protection.

Jesus' teaches his disciples here that prayer is a powerful tool to move the power of God to do God's will. A faithful person's prayer will bring God's will into one's life or the lives of those for whom the prayer is offered.

Then there's one more thing Jesus teaches: a praying person's heart must be clean of unforgiveness. Before praying for your need, forgive those who have sinned against you. Ask God to cleanse your heart. Then pray, "Lord, your will be done…"

Pause and consider is your praying heart a faith-filled clean heart?

A Good Place to Be

What Authority?

> Mark 11:27-28 *They arrived again in Jerusalem, and while Jesus was walking in the temple courts, the chief priests, the teachers of the law and the elders came to him. 28 "By what authority are you doing these things?" they asked. "And who gave you authority to do this?"*

THE DaY after his temple cleansing, Jesus is "walking in the temple courts". Possibly he has come to teach in the space the livestock and merchants have vacated. There is now physical room for him to teach and preach.

Unfortunately, though, more spiritual warfare confronts him. The temple authorities want to know where Jesus, the rabbi, gets the authority to cleanse the temple and to overrule them.

Do you ever feel the teachings in the church are too authoritative, too confrontational over your life? Does a teacher at a Bible study or the pastor in a sermon, or I in these writings, say something that causes you to ask, "Who appointed you judge of my life?" or "Who gave you the authority to tell me what to do?"

If you're asking that question, then you need to go to the Bible to find the answers. God's Word is the authority over your life as you declare Jesus your Lord. Humble yourself. Ask God, "Is this really a sin I must confront?" You must be willing to face your sins if you are to live in God's eternal authority.

Jesus had condemned the temple authorities with his powerful teaching. They objected. No one would tell them how to act! Well, someone did. And that someone is the living Son of God. For the sake of their mortal souls, I hope they humbled themselves before him.

Pause and consider the authority by which you live—yours or Jesus'?

Find Jesus Follow Jesus

Hinge Point

> Mark 11:29-30 Jesus replied, "I will ask you one question. Answer me, and I will tell you by what authority I am doing these things. 30 John's baptism — was it from heaven, or from men? Tell me!"

WHAT'S your response when some person or persons consistently doubts you? Are you frustrated and hurt from their persistent challenges to who you are?

Of course you are, and so is Jesus. He has cleansed the temple of ungodly activity. He has repeatedly shown the miracles of Heaven come to earth. He has preached forgiveness and love. Again and again and again he steps into the public forum to debate the legalists and bring hope to those without hope. All he wants is to love on his people. And all the educated teachers do is say to him in effect, "Who do you think you are? Who gave you the right to cleanse the temple, to judge us and to remove our source of profit?"

Jesus' response is designed to get them to remember their response to John the Baptist. The people of Jerusalem went out into the Jordan to be baptized. John was a popular prophet. People believed him to be the Messiah and that his works were the works of God on earth.

Jesus has drawn a line. If the teachers won't admit John's baptism came from heaven, then what is the point of him telling them, "My authority is from heaven." It's useless to keep preaching to the "deaf".

You probably know that. Some people will never listen to you because they don't want to hear your truth. Question is, are you willing to hear Jesus' truth?

Pause and consider Jesus' has come in the authority of God to speak his truth.

A Good Place to Be

What Do You Choose?

> Mark 11:31-33 They discussed it among themselves and said, "If we say, 'From heaven,' he will ask, 'Then why didn't you believe him?' 32 But if we say, 'From men' . . . ." (They feared the people, for everyone held that John really was a prophet.) 33 So they answered Jesus, "We don't know." Jesus said, "Neither will I tell you by what authority I am doing these things."

DO YOU wonder, "Where is God when I need him? Is Jesus real for me today? I can hardly believe what the Bible says. Savior? I could use some saving right now, Jesus."

Why is it so hard to see Jesus in your life, do you think? Could you possibly be too much like these questioning teachers of Israel? They kept questioning, but they seldom believed. They seemed to always be demanding one more miracle or two more answers or some self-determined sign that Jesus was conforming to their view of life. They did not understand that Jesus came to change their view of life—life "right now" and life eternal.

Jesus walked into their homes, villages, towns, synagogues, cities and temple. He spoke to them of the Kingdom of God, the illustrious wonder of salvation and the joy of forgiveness and love.

But they didn't buy it. Actually, they didn't receive it. They didn't have to buy it. Jesus was *giving* it to them. He was giving all they needed, and they refused it.

There's a deadly truth about people that is deeply disturbing. It goes like this, "When people face change or death, they choose death." It's true, isn't it? Keep up the smoking, drinking, overeating, doing drugs, driving too fast, sexual immorality...ignoring Jesus.

Pause and consider what Jesus gives to you is life for you.

Find Jesus Follow Jesus

The Lord Reigns

Mark 12:1-12 Jesus then began to speak to them in parables: "A man planted a vineyard. He put a wall around it, dug a pit for the winepress and built a watchtower. Then he rented the vineyard to some farmers and went away on a journey. 2 At harvest time he sent a servant to the tenants to collect from them some of the fruit of the vineyard. 3 But they seized him, beat him and sent him away empty-handed. 4 Then he sent another servant to them; they struck this man on the head and treated him shamefully. 5 He sent still another, and that one they killed. He sent many others; some of them they beat, others they killed. 6 "He had one left to send, a son, whom he loved. He sent him last of all, saying, 'They will respect my son.' 7 "But the tenants said to one another, 'This is the heir. Come, let's kill him, and the inheritance will be ours.' 8 So they took him and killed him, and threw him out of the vineyard. 9 "What then will the owner of the vineyard do? He will come and kill those tenants and give the vineyard to others. 10 Haven't you read this scripture: "'The stone the builders rejected has become the capstone; 11 the Lord has done this, and it is marvelous in our eyes'?" 12 Then they looked for a way to arrest him because they knew he had spoken the parable against them. But they were afraid of the crowd; so they left him and went away.

THE TEACHERS acted as the farmers in the parable. They would kill the Son. But the Son reigns over them.

Pause and consider the victory is the Lord's.

A Good Place to Be

God's Inscription

> Mark 12:13-17 *Later they sent some of the Pharisees and Herodians to Jesus to catch him in his words. 14 They came to him and said, "Teacher, we know you are a man of integrity. You aren't swayed by men, because you pay no attention to who they are; but you teach the way of God in accordance with the truth. Is it right to pay taxes to Caesar or not? 15 Should we pay or shouldn't we?" But Jesus knew their hypocrisy. "Why are you trying to trap me?" he asked. "Bring me a denarius and let me look at it." 16 They brought the coin, and he asked them, "Whose portrait is this? And whose inscription?" "Caesar's," they replied. 17 Then Jesus said to them, "Give to Caesar what is Caesar's and to God what is God's." And they were amazed at him.*

WHEN the Bible says in Genesis 1:26 *Then God said, "Let us make man in our image, in our likeness, and let them rule over the fish of the sea and the birds of the air, over the livestock, over all the earth, and over all the creatures that move along the ground."* God is making it clear he has put his mark on every person who is ever born.

Thus, when Jesus says, *"Give to Caesar what is Caesar's and to God what is God's."* he could be talking about money, but it is easy to see he is talking about Kingdom commitment.

"Yes," Jesus says, "pay Caesar his coin. Then give to God what is his—yourself—you."

Made in the image of God, you are stamped with God's image. You are clearly his. Give to him your committed life.

Pause and consider—a coin's image changes. God's does not.

Best is Yet

> Mark 12:18-25 Then the Sadducees, who say there is no resurrection, came to him with a question. 19 "Teacher," they said, "Moses wrote for us that if a man's brother dies and leaves a wife but no children, the man must marry the widow and have children for his brother. 20 Now there were seven brothers. The first one married and died without leaving any children. 21 The second one married the widow, but he also died, leaving no child. It was the same with the third. 22 In fact, none of the seven left any children. Last of all, the woman died too. 23 At the resurrection whose wife will she be, since the seven were married to her?" 24 Jesus replied, "Are you not in error because you do not know the Scriptures or the power of God? 25 When the dead rise, they will neither marry nor be given in marriage; they will be like the angels in heaven."

OFTEN I hear such comments as, "My grandma's blessing me from heaven." "Mom's now together with dad in heaven."

Essentially, those statements are false. A human being entering heaven has no power to look down on the earth and to do anything for anybody. Only one has that power, and he's the Maker of Heaven and earth. People become *like* the angels – they do not become angels – and that means there is no marriage in heaven.

Now, mom and dad can be "together in heaven", but not in the same way they have been on earth. They will have a new kind of relationship, one much better than the best marriage. Know this: heaven is far beyond what you know.

Pause and consider God has reserved the best for forever.

A Good Place to Be

God of the Living

> Mark 12:26-27 Now about the dead rising — have you not read in the book of Moses, in the account of the bush, how God said to him, 'I am the God of Abraham, the God of Isaac, and the God of Jacob'? 27 He is not the God of the dead, but of the living. You are badly mistaken!"

JESUS has been questioned by the Sadducees regarding marriage in heaven. But a much deeper conflict occurs here. The Sadducees do not believe in life after death. Their marriage question was an attempt to trap Jesus into admitting there is no resurrection. As he corrects their thinking on heavenly relationships, he now corrects their error on the resurrection.

And he does so pointing to the Scriptures. As Jesus battled Satan in the wilderness, he now battles Satan's envoys. Jesus resisted the devil with scripture, and he uses the same weapon here.

Jesus reminds the Sadducees God said, *"I am the God of Abraham, the God of Isaac, and the God of Jacob."* As God identifies himself as "I Am", he is saying, "I am the God of Abraham; not only I was so, but I am so; I am the portion and happiness of Abraham, a God all-sufficient to him." (Matthew Henry)

Jesus pointedly proclaimed the Living God to unbelievers whose eyes were clouded by Satan's lies. Although they were experts in the law, they were dead in sin, having no understanding of the eternal God.

Too many "experts" today claim they know all they need to of God. Be careful of what "experts" say.

Pause and consider the only experts on the Father are the Son and Spirit.

Simple, True, Difficult

> Mark 12:28-31 *One of the teachers of the law came and heard them debating. Noticing that Jesus had given them a good answer, he asked him, "Of all the commandments, which is the most important?" 29 "The most important one," answered Jesus, "is this: 'Hear, O Israel, the Lord our God, the Lord is one. 30 Love the Lord your God with all your heart and with all your soul and with all your mind and with all your strength.' 31 The second is this: 'Love your neighbor as yourself.' There is no commandment greater than these."*

JESUS breaks down the Bible into two sentences. Love God. Love your neighbor. Simple, isn't it?

Perhaps it's not simple. If loving God with "*all your mind and with all your strength*" were simple, why don't you do it?

After all, to love God in this way is to have a mind that constantly seeks his truth, using his Word as a filter for everything you say, hear and do. Loving God with your strength is resisting all temptation, protecting your loved ones and standing firm against all who oppose God. Do you do these things?

How easy is it, also, to "Love your neighbor as yourself"? It's not easy at all is it? You readily view your neighbor based on your preferences and point of view. You forget that you're not perfect while expecting your neighbor to be so inclined.

Ah yes, Jesus' breakdown of the biblical truth sounds so simple, but it is very, very difficult to do. "Love" is, indeed, an action word. To obey these commands, you must be a person of action, intentionally turning your heart to love.

Pause and consider those who love you. Is it easy for them?

A Good Place to Be

The Last Question

> Mark 12:32-34 "Well said, teacher," the man replied. "You are right in saying that God is one and there is no other but him. 33 To love him with all your heart, with all your understanding and with all your strength, and to love your neighbor as yourself is more important than all burnt offerings and sacrifices." 34 When Jesus saw that he had answered wisely, he said to him, "You are not far from the kingdom of God." And from then on no one dared ask him any more questions.

DO YOU wonder why Jesus said to the man "You are not far from the kingdom of God?" After all, he had just affirmed Jesus' teachings. His words seem to indicate he is a believer in Jesus, the qualification for Kingdom citizenship.

But as the man affirms Jesus' teachings, he does not indicate a full belief in Jesus, but only the beginning of his faith walk to Jesus. Jesus welcomes him to the beginning of a "kingdom faith" and encourages him to continue his journey.

If you are in a position that has required years of learning, isn't it true you began with a simple faith such as: "If I follow this path, I will become a …" The same is true of attaining the Kingdom of God. If you learn his words and learn who he is, you will be on a path to believe Jesus and who he is. Your statement, "I believe." begins your Kingdom walk. Your walk is strengthened as you walk toward the knowledge of Jesus.

One more thing: Why does "no one dare" to ask Jesus any more questions? They have decided that they are done talking to Jesus. They are determined to kill him.

Sometimes in our despair or uncertainty, we may tire of seeking Jesus. We may feel he's not listening, doesn't care or isn't even there. In despair and frustration, we "kill" Jesus inside of us because we don't like his answers.

Pause and consider: Don't be a Pharisee. Stay with Jesus. He wants to live for you.

The Son is Lord

> Mark 12:35-37 *While Jesus was teaching in the temple courts, he asked, "How is it that the teachers of the law say that the Christ is the son of David? 36 David himself, speaking by the Holy Spirit, declared: (from Psalm110) "'The Lord said to my Lord: "Sit at my right hand until I put your enemies under your feet." 37 David himself calls him 'Lord.' How then can he be his son?" The large crowd listened to him with delight.*

ONE of the Jewish titles for their Messiah is the Son of David, meaning that the Messiah will be a blood descendant of King David. That is the prophecy throughout the Old Testament. Thus, it is correct for the teachers throughout Jewish history to teach that the Messiah would be born to the lineage of David.

Jesus was born from David's bloodline. But now comes Jesus' teaching to elevate the Messiah from the son of an earthly king to the Son of God. As Jesus speaks of David's writings, he is pointing out that David, as a prophet, foretold of the Messiah being his Lord. No earthly descendant would be or could be the earthly Lord of his "father"—his ancestor. Because the Jews believe in the authority of David's prophecies from their scriptures, Jesus is pointing out to them that David's true words of his "son's" lordship because the son comes from the throne of Heaven.

Note the crowd's response. They are delighted. They love hearing the truth because the truth is greater than anything they've ever heard before. They have heard "part" of the gospel story from the prophets' teachings. Now they are beginning to hear the whole story. One day the story will be complete for their salvation.

Pause and consider: Are you delighted the story is complete for your salvation?

A Good Place to Be

Self-focused Teachers

> Mark 12:38-40 as he taught, Jesus said, "Watch out for the teachers of the law. They like to walk around in flowing robes and be greeted in the marketplaces, 39 and have the most important seats in the synagogues and the places of honor at banquets. 40 They devour widows' houses and for a show make lengthy prayers. Such men will be punished most severely."

HYPOCRISY is a great evil in Jesus' eyes. He condemns the Pharisees for the ways they use their status to their advantage. Jesus is particularly harsh as he says they "devour widows' houses". What does he mean by that?

The Pharisees had the authority to exact an excessive tithe of 20-30 per cent from the people. Such a requirement of a widow could make her homeless. Jesus severely condemns this practice. The Son of God often speaks of widows' care as a sign of belief in God. And God's law specifically required the Jews to care for a widow's daily needs. Causing widows to become homeless was clearly a sin.

Now Jesus deals with the sin as he speaks to spiritually "defrock" the ones who wear flowing robes but wear no heart for their people. The Pharisees' pride has become a stumbling block to the heart of God. Jesus calls them out of their hypocrisy into reality. He wants them to be "real" before God, so they will be "real" before his people. The Pharisees have the knowledge to teach people of God's glory. But pridefully they point to their own glory.

This is a grave sin. Keeping people from God will keep the Pharisees from God forever.

Pause and consider: is there any hypocrisy in your heart that might keep someone from God?

Find Jesus Follow Jesus

Looking to Praise

> Mark 12:41-44 *Jesus sat down opposite the place where the offerings were put and watched the crowd putting their money into the temple treasury. Many rich people threw in large amounts. 42 But a poor widow came and put in two very small copper coins, worth only a fraction of a penny. 43 Calling his disciples to him, Jesus said, "I tell you the truth, this poor widow has put more into the treasury than all the others. 44 They all gave out of their wealth; but she, out of her poverty, put in everything — all she had to live on."*

HAVE you ever told a child to do something then watched to see if the child obeyed your command? Of course you have. Why watch them? Are you trying to catch them in disobedience or obedience?

Hopefully your goal is to catch them obeying you, so you can praise them and possibly offer a material reward. But likely your goal was to catch them in their disobedience, so you could correct them.

I think that's why this scripture can make you feel uncomfortable. You don't want people to know what your offering is because it is, if you're like 98% of churched people, too little. You may think Jesus wants to correct those who don't give enough. But is it possible to consider that Jesus is looking for that "heart-giving" person to reward with words of praise and possibly eternal reward? Notice Jesus does not condemn the other givers, but he praises the widow's heart of giving.

This is a good parenting lesson. Praise the obedient child for the heart that honors you. You'll enjoy seeing how easy their obedience will be at your next command.

Pause and consider how joyful it is to praise someone.

A Good Place to Be

Destruction Ahead

> Mark 13:1-3 As he was leaving the temple, one of his disciples said to him, "Look, Teacher! What massive stones! What magnificent buildings!" 2 "Do you see all these great buildings?" replied Jesus. "Not one stone here will be left on another; everyone will be thrown down."

THROUGHOUT Europe there are many magnificent cathedrals and large churches. Some were constructed over centuries of difficult and dangerous labor at great monetary cost to generations of people. Certainly they were indestructible, right?

But walking into these places today, you will learn that some have become museums to a past age. Others are still places where people worship, but they do not nearly fill the space. Crumbling faith in God has caused destruction in God's "houses" around the world.

About 30 years after Jesus spoke these words, Rome came to destroy Jerusalem and fulfill Jesus' prophecy. Why would God allow his house to be so destroyed? He allowed it because the Jews' faith in God had crumbled. The Jews had killed his Son. Jerusalem's religious authorities would not repent. As God had destroyed two previous temples because of his people's unbelief, he did so again.

God will not deal forever with disbelief in and rejection of his Son. What kind of temple is in your heart? Is it a temple of your own beliefs as the Jews created? Or one crumbles with neglect? Or is it a temple of the Living God created in the power of the Holy Spirit?

Build your faith as a testimony to your salvation. Work hard for your sake and for future generations. Pray for the Holy Spirit to make you a temple of the Living God. Strive with all you have to guard it in faith.

Pause and consider how the Living Temple is eternal.

Find Jesus Follow Jesus

See the Signs

> Mark 13:4-8 *"Tell us, when will these things happen? And what will be the sign that they are all about to be fulfilled?" 5 Jesus said to them: "Watch out that no one deceives you. 6 Many will come in my name, claiming, 'I am he,' and will deceive many. 7 When you hear of wars and rumors of wars, do not be alarmed. Such things must happen, but the end is still to come. 8 Nation will rise against nation, and kingdom against kingdom. There will be earthquakes in various places, and famines. These are the beginning of birth pains."*

YOU'VE heard the bad news. "A storm's coming!" You want to know when, don't you? You want to know the details, so you'll be prepared. Maybe, just maybe, you can do something to prepare the storm.

As Jesus prophecies the temple's destruction, the disciples ask the "When?" question. Jesus doesn't tell them specifically when it will be, but he tells them signs they will see as the "Judgment Storm" approaches. Jesus paints a grim picture. Imagine you are Jesus' disciple, and he talks to you of impending doom. What would you do?

Or should I say, "What will you do?" If you call yourself Jesus' disciple, you must listen to Jesus' warnings telling you that wars will rage, earthquakes will destroy, and many false teachers will turn people from Jesus. These things are happening. All creation is scheduled for the final "Judgment Storm". As Jesus' disciples then, you don't know the precise answer to the "When?" question, but you can trust Jesus' words it will occur.

No, you cannot stop the destruction, but if you believe in Jesus' words, you will live in God's new creation. A good Jesus disciple is properly prepared for the storm.

Pause and consider: are you ready?

A Good Place to Be

Spirit's Power

> Mark 13:9-11 *"You must be on your guard. You will be handed over to the local councils and flogged in the synagogues. On account of me you will stand before governors and kings as witnesses to them. 10 And the gospel must first be preached to all nations. 11 Whenever you are arrested and brought to trial, do not worry beforehand about what to say. Just say whatever is given you at the time, for it is not you speaking, but the Holy Spirit."*

YOU see Jesus draw a really grim picture for a Jesus follower, don't you? Who wants that? I do, and here's why: I see the Spirit's power.

When Jesus says, *"Just say whatever is given you at the time, for it is not you speaking, but the Holy Spirit."* Jesus promises his disciples the Holy Spirit will be with them. The promise of the Spirit's presence is an extraordinary promise. The Spirit's presence brings life to you. This is the Spirit that formed the universe at the spoken Word of God! Yes, from the formless void came the world. Into your mind's void comes the power into your mind to know Jesus' truth. Words flow before you can think, and words come before you know what you will say. God's Spirit connects to your spirit; you know God is right there with you!

He gives you vision beyond today's persecution, heartache, joyless days and disappointments to open the eyes of your heart to those around you. You go where you go, do what you do, say what you say because the Holy Spirit pours into you.

Yes, the Spirit is extraordinary power, and he is powerful for you.

Pause and consider God's power is for you.

Find Jesus Follow Jesus

Where's His Love?

> Mark 13:13-14 *"All men will hate you because of me, but he who stands firm to the end will be saved. 14 When you see 'the abomination that causes desolation' standing where it does not belong — let the reader understand — then let those who are in Judea flee to the mountains."*

WHILE I'm looking at this scripture, I'm listening to Alan Jackson's song *"Where Were You" (When the World Stopped Turning)?* The song reflects on the 9/11 twin towers' destruction and reminds us amid the rubble that "Faith, hope and love are some good things (God) gave us, and the greatest is love." Can you really match a God of faith, hope and love with the 9/11 tragedy?

Jesus' prophetic words here foretell Jerusalem's destruction under God's authority. Centuries before Jesus, God used Babylon to destroy his disobedient people and their temple. In 70 A.D., 40 years after Jesus' words here, he used Rome – the new "Babylon" (see *Revelation*) to destroy his disobedient sinful people and the temple that refused to accept his Son. Rome's soldiers murder priests and then destroy the temple. It will be a terrible, terrible time in Jerusalem.

Why? The truth is that even in his love, God must judge his people's disobedience—you must remember that. God is pure. Even as he offers faith, hope and love, God ultimately will destroy the disobedient. In his love, Jesus tells his people then how to save themselves.

That message of "repent and be saved" comes from a loving God, who tells you how to be saved. If you do not repent of your disobedience, even in his love, God will judge you into eternal destruction.

Was 9/11 an act of God's judgment? I don't know. I know evil caused people to die that day. I know people that day entered eternal life because of their faith in a God of hope and love.

Pause and consider faith, hope and love defeat evil.

A Good Place to Be

Jesus' Prayer Request

> Mark 13:18-20 *Pray that this will not take place in winter, 19 because those will be days of distress unequaled from the beginning, when God created the world, until now — and never to be equaled again. 20 If the Lord had not cut short those days, no one would survive. But for the sake of the elect, whom he has chosen, he has shortened them.*

DO YOU see Jesus' "prayer request" here? Or perhaps you could say Jesus is strongly encouraging the people to pray for something specific.

And notice, Jesus doesn't say to pray that God will not destroy the temple and Jerusalem. Destruction is sure. God, the Father, has declared it to the Son, and Jesus prophesies God's sure judgment. But Jesus does say there is something that praying could change amid the sure destruction.

Jesus "prayer request" is that the judgment will not come in winter. Leading up to this, he has warned that people will flee to the mountains and hide in caves. The winter's cold would add more misery to the horrible events. As he prophesies destruction, Jesus is also offering priestly advice to pray for some measure of comfort and care amid the destruction.

The same is true for you. Jesus came as a prophet to teach the Gospel truth. He prophesies you will face God's judgment one day. Jesus also came as a priest to save you from the Father's sure judgment. In his death for you, he takes the Father's judgment upon himself. When you receive him as Lord, you receive the benefits of his prophetic teaching. You also receive the benefits of his priestly sacrifice for you.

Pray for protection in the impending judgment, and you will be saved.

Pause and consider the power of prayer to save.

Permanent Shield

> Mark 13:21-23 "At that time if anyone says to you, 'Look, here is the Christ!' or, 'Look, there he is!' do not believe it. 22 For false Christs and false prophets will appear and perform signs and miracles to deceive the elect — if that were possible. 23 So be on your guard; I have told you everything ahead of time."

THE BIBLE gives to you many pictures of God's constant, protective care over you. For example, God promises in Isaiah 61:3 that those he chooses or elects *"will be called oaks of righteousness, a planting of the Lord for the display of his splendor."* Although much will come against those who receive salvation, they will stand tall and sturdy to display God's glory.

In a similar fashion, Jesus tells the elect that they will survive the terrible judgment at the end of time. He warns the trial will include false teachers trying to persuade the elect to turn from Jesus, the true Messiah. These false teachers will even have ability to do miracles under the permission of the Father. This will be a testing, and Jesus assures the elect they will remain under the Father's protection.

Jesus offers you two key lessons. First, be prepared to know the difference between the false and the true teachers of God's Word. Look around, and you'll quickly see how liars prevail upon the innocent as they add their own words to God's Word. You must know God's Word to warn those who do not yet confess Christ.

Your second lesson is to live courageously and confidently in God's Word. You may be attacked because you are the Lord's elect, but you will stand the victor when the trials are done. In the dark days, look to "the Light of the World". (John 8:12)

Pause and consider God's truth protects and saves.

A Good Place to Be

Scene Shift

> Mark 13:24-29 "But in those days, following that distress, 'the sun will be darkened, and the moon will not give its light; 25 the stars will fall from the sky, and the heavenly bodies will be shaken.' 26 At that time men will see the Son of Man coming in clouds with great power and glory. 27 And he will send his angels and gather his elect from the four winds, from the ends of the earth to the ends of the heavens. 28 Now learn this lesson from the fig tree: As soon as its twigs get tender and its leaves come out, you know that summer is near. 29 Even so, when you see these things happening, you know that it is near, right at the door."

DO YOU see the words "*in those days, following that distress*"? Jesus shifts his warnings from the impending judgment on Jerusalem in the near future to the final Day of Judgment as the Father forms the new Heaven and new earth. (2 Peter 3:13 *But in keeping with his promise we are looking forward to a new heaven and a new earth, the home of righteousness.*)

Jesus will come with great power and glory to establish his reign over God's new creation. See how he promises to gather his elect to him. In this promise is also a warning that one's doom is sure outside of his elect.

This is the 7th time I've shared with you Jesus' warnings to his people of the Father's judgment. He will end all sin one day to restore his perfect creation. Your loving God has clearly described an end to life as you know it. Are you listening?

Pause and consider how sure is the end...are you sure of your status at the end?

Find Jesus Follow Jesus

Watch!

> Mark 13:30-37 *I tell you the truth, this generation will certainly not pass away until all these things have happened. 31 Heaven and earth will pass away, but my words will never pass away. 32 "No one knows about that day or hour, not even the angels in heaven, nor the Son, but only the Father. 33 Be on guard! Be alert! You do not know when that time will come. 34 It's like a man going away: He leaves his house and puts his servants in charge, each with his assigned task, and tells the one at the door to keep watch. 35 "Therefore keep watch because you do not know when the owner of the house will come back — whether in the evening, or at midnight, or when the rooster crows, or at dawn. 36 If he comes suddenly, do not let him find you sleeping. 37 What I say to you, I say to everyone: 'Watch!'"*

IF YOU knew for certain that someone was going to come into your house to threaten your family and your life, you would be on the watch, wouldn't you? You would prepare as thoroughly as you could to save your family, yourself and your home from destruction. You would be on the watch, posting all the latest technology and knowledge available to you to know as soon as possible when the invader is coming. In all ways possible you would be awake to recoil the destruction.

Are you doing all you can to guard your soul against God's judgment? Are you "watching" what you read, "watching" what you hear, and "watching" what you believe? Are you "watching" your heart? Are you "watching" your loved ones' hearts to guard and strengthen them?

Pause and consider you must be an alert "watcher".

A Good Place to Be

Cowards

> Mark 14:1-2 Now the Passover and the Feast of Unleavened Bread were only two days away, and the chief priests and the teachers of the law were looking for some sly way to arrest Jesus and kill him. 2 "But not during the Feast," they said, "or the people may riot."

WHY would the priests and teachers hide their actions? What guilt and shame defiled their heart! If Jesus were such a terrible threat to the Jews and to the nation, why didn't they publicly arrest him? Surely they had the power of Rome on their side to keep the peace.

Truth is, they knew the truth, and they wanted to kill the truth. They knew Jesus had spoken truth in all he taught. They had no reply to his truth. They gave up trying to trick him because he made fools of them. Jesus exposed their lies and their false motives. Only one thing motivated them—their love of power.

What motivates you? Are you ready to "kill" Jesus because you have no reply to his truth?

Yes, you can kill Jesus by avoiding him and what he teaches. Think of lessons you learned in school long ago. Actually, you can't, can you? You've forgotten much of what you learned to pass the tests and to get your diploma. You retain only the information you use. You've killed the other stuff by neglecting it and not using it.

Jesus' truth is what you need in your life each day. Are you feeling guilt and shame for killing Jesus? Then pray to him, and ask him to revive, to make his truth come alive in you.

Pause and consider you must keep the truth alive in you.

Find Jesus Follow Jesus

Love Legacy

> Mark 14:3-9 *While he was in Bethany, reclining at the table in the home of a man known as Simon the Leper, a woman came with an alabaster jar of very expensive perfume, made of pure nard. She broke the jar and poured the perfume on his head. 4 Some of those present were saying indignantly to one another, "Why this waste of perfume? 5 It could have been sold for more than a year's wages and the money given to the poor." And they rebuked her harshly. 6 "Leave her alone," said Jesus. "Why are you bothering her? She has done a beautiful thing to me. 7 The poor you will always have with you, and you can help them any time you want. But you will not always have me. 8 She did what she could. She poured perfume on my body beforehand to prepare for my burial. 9 I tell you the truth, wherever the gospel is preached throughout the world, what she has done will also be told, in memory of her."*

WHAT DO YOU remember most about people who have loved you? You remember how they showed their love for you. Even when romances break up, after the heartache or even anger have left your heart, you still have a place to remember how they loved you.

A woman pours out her love to Jesus through the perfume. Think of her sacrifice. She had poured out a year's income on Jesus. Perhaps she was wealthy, but if she were, she likely loved money. She found she loved her Lord more. If she were poor, she truly offered a life sacrifice.

Apparently the others' loved the money more. They berated her. But Jesus effectively said, "Stop it. She loves me. Do you?"

Pause and consider your answer.

A Good Place to Be

Betrayal

> Mark 14:10-11 Then Judas Iscariot, one of the Twelve, went to the chief priests to betray Jesus to them. 11 They were delighted to hear this and promised to give him money. So he watched for an opportunity to hand him over.

"BETRAYAL" is a terrible sin, isn't it? If you want to hurt someone, betray their trust in you. They'll harbor hard feelings against you for a very long time, perhaps for the rest of their lives. Betrayal is so hard to forgive. Why do people betray those who love them? Why would Judas betray Jesus?

Perhaps the simplest answer was Judas' greed. He bartered his rabbi's life for 33 pieces of silver. Or maybe he thought Jesus was blaspheming—betraying—God and deserved death. Maybe he was disappointed that Jesus had failed to take military action to overthrow Rome. Regardless of his reasons, he betrayed Jesus for his own reason. He had no regard for anyone else.

That's the way betrayal works. Someone becomes motivated more about "me" than "we". Betrayers put their own priorities above the relationship. You may feel superior or inadequate to the other, making a one-sided decision about the relationship or some aspect of the relationship.

For example, a teen-aged driver betrays his parents' trust to drive the car when he hides the truth of a speeding ticket. His main concern is "me" – that they continue to let him drive. Truth hides in the "back seat". Honesty is relegated to "the trunk". When dad opens "the trunk" to discover the truth, he feels betrayed. The father-son relationship suffers until forgiveness restores the relationship.

Do you betray Jesus? Do you call him Lord, and then put his truths "in the trunk"?

Pause and consider Jesus checks the trunk all the time. Seek his forgiveness.

Find Jesus Follow Jesus

The Truth

> Mark 14:16-18 *The disciples left, went into the city and found things just as Jesus had told them. So they prepared the Passover. 17 When evening came, Jesus arrived with the Twelve. 18 While they were reclining at the table eating, he said, "I tell you the truth, one of you will betray me — one who is eating with me."*

JESUS commonly said, "I tell you the truth." This was a powerful phrase for his disciples and all who heard it. To some it was a phrase of arrogance and superiority.

You see, when the teachers taught from the scrolls, they would correctly say, "The Lord says." or "The scrolls say." All who correctly teach Jesus' truth today must quote the truth. God's truth comes directly only from the Father, Son and Spirit.

As Jesus said, "I tell you the truth." he is proclaiming his Lordship. He speaks an absolute truth. To adjust his truth or refuse his truth, you are refusing his Lordship.

When he proclaims at his last Passover supper, "*I tell you the truth, one of you will betray me — one who is eating with me.*" he speaks a new and hard truth to his disciples. As the disciples heard his words of death and resurrection, his "truth talk" must have put fear into their hearts, and it must have stirred Judas to action.

The disciples fearfully ate their meal, wondering, "Will Jesus' awful warnings about his death come true?" Certainly they hoped otherwise. But the truth is, they would come to know that the betrayal of Jesus was a truth that would ultimately set them free.

Pause and consider all God's truth works to your salvation.

A Good Place to Be

Surely Not I

> Mark 14:19-21 They were saddened, and one by one they said to him, "Surely not I?" 20 "It is one of the Twelve," he replied, "one who dips bread into the bowl with me. 21 The Son of Man will go just as it is written about him. But woe to that man who betrays the Son of Man! It would be better for him if he had not been born."

OH, THE HURT! Here is Jesus sharing the Passover meal to remember the Lord's extraordinary gift of freedom from Egypt. A devout Jew considers this one of the holiest nights of the year—similar to our feelings on Christmas and Easter.

When you look at Jesus' words here, you must understand how deeply Jesus felt the wound of betrayal in his heart, especially on this holy, intimate night. When he spoke "*it is one of the Twelve*", he was clearly telling his closest students, the ones *he* had chosen, that one of them would betray him.

How painful was his soul to admit this truth and to know the man, Judas, would be condemned to Hell. How deep was the grief in Jesus' heart as he looked into the face of his beloved disciple and said, "Woe to that man."

Think about Judas' fate, and then tell me it is okay to betray Jesus. Betrayal is eternally deadly, and you must stop it. You must also speak to others to tell them this truth. If your destiny is Hell, indeed, it would have been better for you not to have been born.

Out of the deep emotions of the Passover meal, Jesus mourns his friend's future. How would he view your future?

Pause and consider your answer. Remember Jesus loves you to keep you from woe.

Communion

> Mark 14:22-25 While they were eating, Jesus took bread, gave thanks and broke it, and gave it to his disciples, saying, "Take it; this is my body." 23 Then he took the cup, gave thanks and offered it to them, and they all drank from it. 24 "This is my blood of the covenant, which is poured out for many," he said to them. 25 "I tell you the truth, I will not drink again of the fruit of the vine until that day when I drink it anew in the kingdom of God."

OH MY. How deep the Father's love for you that he would send his Son to commune with mankind on earth, then to establish a way you can commune with him through your life right now that you may finally enter into Heaven, where you can commune with Jesus forever.

As you think of communion, I pray you think of Jesus' offering to you—his broken body and his shed blood. He sat that night in a ceremony similar to a Jewish betrothal when a man raised his glass of wine to commit his life to his bride. He makes a life commitment, offering himself to care for her as long as he lives.

Jesus broke the bread, and he raised the cup. Then he said, "This is for you." Grab hold of that and live in joy! His death is for your life if you but receive the cup and the bread from him.

Yes, when you take communion in church, you are literally taking hold of elements that represent Jesus body and blood. Consider this gratefully. The God of creation offers his very essence to you to save you!

Pause and consider how eternal it is to commune with Jesus. Then be thankful.

| A Good Place to Be

Jesus Sang

> Mark 14:26 When they had sung a hymn, they went out to the Mount of Olives.

DID you know Jesus sang with his disciples? I mentioned this verse to someone, and the surprised person asked, "They sang a hymn?" I wonder what Jesus' range was. Did Jesus have perfect pitch? Maybe he sang lead. Or perhaps Jesus sang supporting harmony. He was very good, I'm sure, in either role.

What did they sing? After a meal, it was customary for the Jews to sings psalms from the *Hallel*—a name for Psalms 113-118. Read through them and you will see many familiar phrases of praise to God, e.g.

Psalms 116:1-6 I love the Lord, for he heard my voice; he heard my cry for mercy. 2 Because he turned his ear to me, I will call on him as long as I live. 3 The cords of death entangled me, the anguish of the grave came upon me; I was overcome by trouble and sorrow. 4 Then I called on the name of the Lord: "O Lord, save me!" 5 The Lord is gracious and righteous; our God is full of compassion. 6 The Lord protects the simplehearted; when I was in great need, he saved me.

Psalms 118:1 Give thanks to the Lord, for he is good; his love endures forever.

Verse upon verse of the *Hallel* proclaim God's salvation. Several have been incorporated into modern praise songs. Many have been used in hymns and calls to worship through the centuries. Jesus and his disciples sang on that emotional distressing night and received comfort. Isn't it good to know God has gifted artists through the centuries to use his word to comfort you?

Pause and consider how God's music is so good for you.

Find Jesus Follow Jesus

Shepherd's Care

> Mark 14:27-28 *"You will all fall away," Jesus told them, "for it is written: "'I will strike the shepherd, and the sheep will be scattered.' 28 But after I have risen, I will go ahead of you into Galilee."*

HOW would you feel if someone wrote in a book about 20 years ago that God would strike you (specifically using your name) with sudden death at the hands of your enemies, scattering your family and friends, putting them at risk. I wonder if you'd say anything. I'm not sure I would. I'd probably avoid talking about it, hoping God changed his mind.

About 500 years before Jesus, the prophet Zechariah wrote (13:7) *"Awake, O sword, against my shepherd, against the man who is close to me!" declares the Lord Almighty. "Strike the shepherd, and the sheep will be scattered, and I will turn my hand against the little ones."*

Now, instead of hiding or avoiding the Father's purpose for his life, Jesus embraces it. He has prepared for his death at the Last Supper. He sang praise to God. He goes now to Gethsemane to prepare to meet his betrayer and the evil he brings with him. Jesus does not shirk from his God-ordained purpose. He embraces it.

And he encourages his disciples, *"But after I have risen, I will go ahead of you into Galilee."* At this hour of grief, Jesus remains the Good Shepherd. In the crisis of impending crucifixion, Jesus comforts and assures his disciples that the pain, grief and death are only temporary, but a mere few hours. Then he will come alive and meet up with them again.

The Good Shepherd meets his purpose. The Good Shepherd assures his flock. The Good Shepherd shows faith.

Pause and consider your response to God's purpose for you.

A Good Place to Be

Peter's Four Denials

> *Mark 14:29-31 Peter declared, "Even if all fall away, I will not." 30 "I tell you the truth," Jesus answered, "today — yes, tonight — before the rooster crows twice you yourself will disown me three times." 31 But Peter insisted emphatically, "Even if I have to die with you, I will never disown you." And all the others said the same.*

I KNOW. You're saying, "Peter didn't deny Jesus four times." And so it was as recorded in Scripture.

But let's consider Peter's words to Jesus in this Scripture. Jesus said, *"I tell you the truth…you yourself will disown me three times."* What's true when Jesus said, "I tell you the truth"? Of course, what he said was true.

But Peter denied Jesus' truth here. *"I will never disown you."* He said. Peter, my friend, arguing with the Truth is futile. Wouldn't it have been better for you to go into prayer about what Jesus had said? Wouldn't you want to find strength to get through the trial you were about to face? Wouldn't you pray for the Father to guard your heart amid the hurt that was about to happen? Wouldn't you have sought the Lord's strength to endure the agony of denying your Lord?

Peter, you good man, why were you so eager to argue with Jesus? He's your rabbi. You've seen him do miracles. You've seen his glory on the mount. You've heard him chastise the Pharisees for their unbelief. Peter! Wake up and see what the sovereign Lord has purposed for you. I know you don't like this purpose. Jesus certainly didn't like going to the cross, but he said, "Yes, Father." But, Peter, All you can say is "No, Lord."

Pause and consider, Peter, you need to figure out who's Lord of your life.

Grief

> Mark 14:32-35 They went to a place called Gethsemane, and Jesus said to his disciples, "Sit here while I pray." 33 He took Peter, James and John along with him, and he began to be deeply distressed and troubled. 34 "My soul is overwhelmed with sorrow to the point of death," he said to them. "Stay here and keep watch." 35 Going a little farther, he fell to the ground and prayed that if possible the hour might pass from him.

JESUS' extreme grief here is the result of his impending separation from the Father and the Spirit. The Holy Trinity was to be divided to mend sin's division. Perhaps it is easy to say, "His separation was only for 3 days. That's nothing." But that view erases the truth of Jesus' grievous emotional experience in Gethsemane.

Consider the Holy Trinity is the eternal, self-existent God. The mystery of God, three-in-one is a reality we scarcely comprehend. And as Jesus is separated from the Trinity, even if it is a blip in eternity, the Trinity will experience a deep grief surpassing all knowledge. You can't imagine, can you, how grief-stricken you would be if you had to kill your child—even if it were just for an instant knowing he would come back to life. You couldn't do it. You would prefer to kill yourself or run from your obligation. You would consider no cause worthwhile to cause you to do such a horrible thing.

Yes, this is not Jesus going away for a weekend to return to work on Sunday morning. The Father is about to kill the Son. And the Spirit makes it happen. The Holy Trinity's deep grief shows forth in Jesus' grieving heart.

Pause and consider how grievous is your sin to cause Jesus' death.

A Good Place to Be

Strength Needed

> Mark 14:36-40 *"Abba, Father," he said, "everything is possible for you. Take this cup from me. Yet not what I will, but what you will." 37 Then he returned to his disciples and found them sleeping. "Simon," he said to Peter, "are you asleep? Could you not keep watch for one hour? 38 Watch and pray so that you will not fall into temptation. The spirit is willing, but the body is weak." 39 Once more he went away and prayed the same thing. 40 When he came back, he again found them sleeping, because their eyes were heavy. They did not know what to say to him.*

YOU get that way, don't you? When you know you've failed Jesus, you don't know what to say to him. Jesus' disciples have failed him again at this 11th hour. He asked them to pray for themselves and for him, but they have fallen asleep. Even pompous fight-to-the-death Peter is sleeping.

This picture is too real for me. I consider the times I have failed my Lord as I've failed to pray for me in my calling, for his workers—his missionaries, pastors, Sunday school teachers, and churches. I've failed to pray for the Spirit to come and work his power on unrepentant souls. I've failed to pray in faith for healing in our community and healing in our bodies. I've failed to pray for revival.

I've been too busy sleeping, worn out from my labor because I labor too much without the Spirit. I deny my Lord when I say I will defend him. I go with him to hard places, but my weak flesh retreats to the tree, and I fall asleep.

I wonder what it would be like if I prayed for the Spirit's strength?

Pause and consider the Spirit's strength is for you.

Find Jesus Follow Jesus

The Kiss

> Mark 14: 41-45 *Returning the third time, he said to them, "Are you still sleeping and resting? Enough! The hour has come. Look, the Son of Man is betrayed into the hands of sinners. 42 Rise! Let us go! Here comes my betrayer!" 43 Just as he was speaking, Judas, one of the Twelve, appeared. With him was a crowd armed with swords and clubs, sent from the chief priests, the teachers of the law, and the elders. 44 Now the betrayer had arranged a signal with them: "The one I kiss is the man; arrest him and lead him away under guard." 45 Going at once to Jesus, Judas said, "Rabbi!" and kissed him.*

HAVE YOU seen such an unholy kiss? Judas, you betrayer, you've done your dirty work. You've brought to Gethsemane a crowd of people who will follow the crowd, regardless of where it goes even if it goes to Hell. What are you thinking? What are the disciples thinking when they see you kiss their rabbi?

You call him, "Rabbi!" but really he is no longer your rabbi. You've turned on him, and you've turned him in. You brought along some cowards who have only courage to arrest Jesus in the dark. Evil works at night, Judas, and you're leading the way.

How could you do this, Judas? What do you think of Jesus standing there to receive your kiss? What is it like when your lips touched his cheek? Does he back off to repulse you? Do you have any regrets, Judas? Do you wonder why you answered his call to follow? Do you feel hollow inside? Do you perhaps want to turn and defend him? Or is it too late?

Pause and consider it's not too late to give your Lord a holy kiss.

A Good Place to Be

Running Time

> Mark 14:46-50 *The men seized Jesus and arrested him. 47 Then one of those standing near drew his sword and struck the servant of the high priest, cutting off his ear. 48 "Am I leading a rebellion," said Jesus, "that you have come out with swords and clubs to capture me? 49 Every day I was with you, teaching in the temple courts, and you did not arrest me. But the Scriptures must be fulfilled." 50 Then everyone deserted him and fled.*

MR. DISCIPLES, you fled? I thought you were *disciplined*, willing to stay with your Lord when the hard things happened. You said you were ready to die with him. (Matt 26:35) Peter, you said so this very night.

Do you remember, Mr. Disciples, how Jesus aggressively confronted the teachers of the law? Do you recall how he had faithfully healed on the Sabbath, even though he was repeatedly criticized? You remember, don't you, how Jesus had passionately cleansed the temple? You even showed some courage leaving your homes and your jobs to follow Jesus. Why are you fleeing now?

Conflict is scary, isn't it, Mr. Disciples? You expect when you're following the Lord that everything will be easy. You thought you'd be sitting at his right and left hand by now, didn't you James and John? But something is amiss. Something is wrong, horribly wrong, and you don't know what to do about it. One thing you surely won't do, though, is stay in the battle alongside your Lord. That's too much to ask, isn't it?

Don't feel badly, guys. Fear has sent most of us running from Jesus one time or another. Some of us run all the time. We stand for nothing, and we have no faith.

Pause and consider fear is a faithless factor.

Find Jesus Follow Jesus

Peter's Purpose

> Mark 14:51-54 *A young man, wearing nothing but a linen garment, was following Jesus. When they seized him, 52 he fled naked, leaving his garment behind. 53 They took Jesus to the high priest, and all the chief priests, elders and teachers of the law came together. 54 Peter followed him at a distance, right into the courtyard of the high priest. There he sat with the guards and warmed himself at the fire.*

WHEN Peter walked into the courtyard, do you think his intentions were good? I think so. I believe he went there to see what they would do to Jesus. I believe he went there ready to defend Jesus, and based on his words in Gethsemane, I believe he went there ready to die. His good intentions were to defend his good Master.

Sitting around the fire, he must have watched and waited. He may even have planned a way to free Jesus from this mockery. He was a fisherman, a country boy. He certainly had fought a time or two. He certainly was muscular. He was a guy who did things, took matters into his hands. He moved confidently and boldly. That was his life. Why wouldn't he be that way now?

Could it be God had other plans for this man? Of course he did, and those plans were to join the other Apostles to begin the church, to spread the Good News, to use his boldness to defend Jesus in another way, an eternal way.

Of course, Peter had no such thoughts that night. He was ready—or so he thought—for immediate action to save Jesus. Little did he know that God would save him that night to save others.

Pause and consider God's plan really is much better for you.

A Good Place to Be

What to Say?

> *Mark 14:55-60 The chief priests and the whole Sanhedrin were looking for evidence against Jesus so that they could put him to death, but they did not find any. 56 Many testified falsely against him, but their statements did not agree. 57 Then some stood up and gave this false testimony against him: 58 "We heard him say, 'I will destroy this man-made temple and in three days will build another, not made by man.'" 59 Yet even then their testimony did not agree. 60 Then the high priest stood up before them and asked Jesus, "Are you not going to answer? What is this testimony that these men are bringing against you?"*

DO YOU wonder at Jesus' silence, why he didn't speak to defend himself? Let me ask you this. Have you ever spoken plainly and truthfully about something, and no one believed you? Perhaps you recognized a new manufacturing method. You told the boss and all around you what would work better. But no one listened. What did you do? Likely, you stopped talking. More words were fruitless.

Jesus had come to bear the fruit of the Kingdom of God, but few listened to him. Jesus had plainly spoken Kingdom truths before these men who sought to kill him. He now plainly knew they had no desire to seek the true way. Their desire was to put him away.

And so it is with you. You hear Jesus' truth. Would he give up speaking to you? Is your purpose to stay in your ways and to put Jesus away? He calls you to account. He calls you to action. He calls you to salvation. Why don't you let him speak?

Pause and consider Jesus is speaking to save you.

Son of Man Speaks

> Mark 14:61 *But Jesus remained silent and gave no answer. Again the high priest asked him, "Are you the Christ, the Son of the Blessed One?" 62 "I am," said Jesus. "And you will see the Son of Man sitting at the right hand of the Mighty One and coming on the clouds of heaven."*

TO DANIEL, God gave this vision of God's final judgment on earth: *Daniel 7:13-14 "I looked, and there before me was one like a son of man, coming with the clouds of heaven. He approached the Ancient of Days and was led into his presence. 14 He was given authority, glory and sovereign power; all peoples, nations and men of every language worshiped him. His dominion is an everlasting dominion that will not pass away, and his kingdom is one that will never be destroyed."*

Caiaphas, the high priest questioning Jesus, knew exactly how Jesus was answering his question, *"Are you the Christ, the Son of the Blessed One?"*

When Jesus said, *"And you will see the Son of Man sitting at the right hand of the Mighty One and coming on the clouds of heaven."* he was speaking the message Daniel had received from Heaven. When Jesus responded with his "Son of Man" language, Caiaphas understands he is claiming to be the Son of God, who will establish his throne on earth.

Jesus has consistently used the prophets' words to affirm he is the Messiah. People have believed him or condemned him. It seems as if Jesus may be giving Caiaphas one last opportunity to believe him.

In fact, he may be giving his people one last opportunity to believe him. He has clearly spoken the truth, but few have believed.

Pause over what you have heard from Jesus and consider your belief in him.

Ignorant

> Mark 14:63-66 The high priest tore his clothes. "Why do we need any more witnesses?" he asked. 64 "You have heard the blasphemy. What do you think?" They all condemned him as worthy of death. 65 Then some began to spit at him; they blindfolded him, struck him with their fists, and said, "Prophesy!" And the guards took him and beat him.

BLASPHEMY is evil, mocking speech against God. The priest tears his clothes to show he separates himself from the sin.

Of course, Jesus had not spoken blasphemy. He had spoken the truth. The real blasphemy occurs here in the priests' and teachers' litany of evil, mocking speech against the Holy Lord. These ignorant men are digging a deep hole of words that mock God, and one day they will be condemned.

It's odd, isn't it? These men accuse Jesus of blasphemy. But Jesus is innocent, and they are guilty. Let's consider why they act in such ignorance.

Where do ignorant acts come from? They come from minds empty of the truth. I know you might think the word "ignorant" is a harsh, judgmental word, but often it's good to have a "wake up" word to get you to think about it. When I consider how ignorant I am regarding Jesus, I am driven to fill more of him into my mind. When I see how the world today is ignorant of Jesus, I mourn the ignorance, and I strive to teach as many as I can. All of our minds are too empty of the knowledge of Jesus Christ. The truth is we must mourn our own ignorance. We must mourn others' ignorance.

Jesus knew ignorance kills. Do you think he mourned his accusers?

Pause and consider that you cannot ignore ignorance.

Find Jesus Follow Jesus

Time to Change?

> Mark 14:67-72 When she saw Peter warming himself, she looked closely at him. "You also were with that Nazarene, Jesus," she said. 68 But he denied it. "I don't know or understand what you're talking about," he said, and went out into the entryway. 69 When the servant girl saw him there, she said again to those standing around, "This fellow is one of them." 70 Again he denied it. After a little while, those standing near said to Peter, "Surely you are one of them, for you are a Galilean." 71 He began to call down curses on himself, and he swore to them, "I don't know this man you're talking about." 72 Immediately the rooster crowed the second time. Then Peter remembered the word Jesus had spoken to him: "Before the rooster crows twice you will disown me three times." And he broke down and wept.

DO YOU find Peter perplexing? He's such a passionate man. He loves Jesus so very much. He is willing to defend his rabbi's life. He's likely in this place to try to help Jesus. He follows Jesus into the "devil's lair". Certainly he is a man of courage. What happened to him?

Was he afraid? Was he embarrassed? Was he at a loss about what to do, how to behave? Was he so upset he didn't know what he was doing? Was he too much like you and me?

You know about promising Jesus your life and giving him your denial, don't you? We're good at that. You commit to Jesus as your Lord and Savior, and then you submit to your old habits. After all the bravado and promises of, "Jesus, I love you." you look change in the face. Suddenly it looks easier to deny Jesus than follow him.

Pause and consider Jesus change is life change. Then do it.

A Good Place to Be

The King is Silent

> Mark 15:1-5 *Very early in the morning, the chief priests, with the elders, the teachers of the law and the whole Sanhedrin, reached a decision. They bound Jesus, led him away and handed him over to Pilate. 2 "Are you the king of the Jews?" asked Pilate. "Yes, it is as you say," Jesus replied. 3 The chief priests accused him of many things. 4 So again Pilate asked him, "Aren't you going to answer? See how many things they are accusing you of."* 5 But Jesus still made no reply, and Pilate was amazed.

ARE YOU amazed at Jesus' silence? Wouldn't this be a good time for Jesus to find an ally in Pilate? After all, Pilate can save him from the brutal cross.

Is Jesus' silence, perhaps, fatalism because he knows his destiny is the cross? Is he thinking, "Why bother? I'm just going to die anyway. The Father's will is that I go to the cross. So I'll just keep quiet. I'd hate to be set free if I'm supposed to die."

If Jesus had thought that, he would have been a self-serving fatalist. Such thoughts point to one's own glory, and in essence say, "Look at how good I am to suffer."

Yes, the truth is that the Father has ordained Jesus' suffering, and Jesus responds as the true Son of God. He humbly submits to God's divine plan to reveal God's glory through his suffering.

Every time Jesus spoke of his suffering to his disciples, he spoke in the third person, i. e. "The Son of Man must be killed." He pointed away from himself to the prophets and to God, that the Father would be glorified.

Pause and consider Jesus' humble submission.

Find Jesus Follow Jesus

Whatever!

> Mark 15:6-11 *Now it was the custom at the Feast to release a prisoner whom the people requested. 7 A man called Barabbas was in prison with the insurrectionists who had committed murder in the uprising. 8 The crowd came up and asked Pilate to do for them what he usually did. 9 "Do you want me to release to you the king of the Jews?" asked Pilate, 10 knowing it was out of envy that the chief priests had handed Jesus over to him. 11 But the chief priests stirred up the crowd to have Pilate release Barabbas instead.*

YOU'VE been there. You must make a decision you'd rather give to someone else. Perhaps it's a matter regarding finances or a household dispute. I guess the "irresponsible" phrase today is "Whatever!" and you just walk away thinking, "Whatever! I'm not responsible. Don't blame me for this."

Pilate's a "Whatever!" guy who wants to find a way out of condemning Jesus to death. The thing is, Pilate had a really good way out. He had the power to simply release Jesus. He didn't need anyone's approval. He was *the man!* But instead, Pilate acted the "Whatever! Man".

He wanted to be politically correct. He didn't want to look bad to the Jews. He didn't want to seem weak to the Romans. He was used to killing people. What's one more, even if it's wrong? Maybe he could save Jesus in the culture's way.

The horrible truth is, Pilate's "Whatever!" is still killing Jesus. You'd rather not be responsible to tell the truth against the culture's accusations.

The truth is, though, you can be sure and strong to defend Jesus. You have the power of his Truth.

Pause and consider this "whatever": Colossians 3:17 And whatever you do...do it all in the name of the Lord Jesus.

A Good Place to Be

What Did You Say?

> Mark 15:12-14 "What shall I do, then, with the one you call the king of the Jews?" Pilate asked them. 13 "Crucify him!" they shouted. 14 "Why? What crime has he committed?" asked Pilate. But they shouted all the louder, "Crucify him!"

DO YOU wonder if those people had any idea what they were saying? Yes, of course, they knew what crucifixion was. They knew if Pilate listened to them, Jesus would die. But do you think they knew what they were saying?

Consider for example some of the things you might say. You angrily shout to someone you love, "Shut up!" You tell your kids in a loud voice, "Don't you ever do that again." You impatiently tell your wife, "I'll get it done!" as you leave the house the night after you've expressed love to her. You tell your kids, "I know I promised, but…"

Do you have any idea what you're saying? The crowd's words called to kill Jesus, and they had no idea how their words brought God's judgment on them. You speak in unloving, impatient, self-focused ways to your family, and you have no idea how your words bring God's judgment on you.

Yes, they do. God is clear, dads about being humble and submissive to your wife—to the point of death!—and not exasperating your children. God is clear, moms, about being humble and submissive to your husbands and not exasperating your children.

I know, God commands your children to honor you. My question is, "Do they have an honorable parent to honor?"

Watch what you say. Always, always find ways to speak encouragement, patience, love and affirmation to your beloved ones, your neighbors and your church. Before you speak, make sure you have an idea you know what you are saying.

Pause and consider your speech.

Mock Worship

> *Mark 15:15-20 Wanting to satisfy the crowd, Pilate released Barabbas to them. He had Jesus flogged, and handed him over to be crucified. 16 The soldiers led Jesus away into the palace (that is, the Praetorium) and called together the whole company of soldiers. 17 They put a purple robe on him, then twisted together a crown of thorns and set it on him. 18 And they began to call out to him, "Hail, king of the Jews!" 19 Again and again they struck him on the head with a staff and spit on him. Falling on their knees, they paid homage to him. 20 And when they had mocked him, they took off the purple robe and put his own clothes on him. Then they led him out to crucify him.*

THOSE horrible soldiers weren't just content to crucify him, they had to mock him first. The thorny crown, the purple robe symbolized the evil and hatred in their hearts.

Their hatred for Jesus was the kind of hatred God's people had shown against God's Law for centuries as they hatefully killed his prophets. Evil was running amok in Israel, Judah and the non-Jewish soldiers. The godly Jews, who desired God's presence and who saw Jesus as their Messiah were shut down. Their voices were weak and silent. Evil – absolute corruption – seems to be the champion of the day.

Yes, that's the way it seems, doesn't it? You hear many types of Jesus-mocking speech in our culture. Evil rules tongues and minds. God-honoring speech is covered over. Sometimes the mocking is our being quiet when we should speak.

Is there any hope to rid the world of this mocking, hateful, God-killing speech? The Hope is on his way to the cross.

Pause and consider, are you in any way mocking God?

A Good Place to Be

The Cross Moment

> Mark 15:21 *A certain man from Cyrene, Simon, the father of Alexander and Rufus, was passing by on his way in from the country, and they forced him to carry the cross.*

THERE YOU are running some errands when suddenly Jesus shows up. Oh, he may look like a stranded motorist, a neighbor who "needs to talk" or a friend who seeks refuge from a busy world. What do you do?

Simon of Cyrene—an ordinary man and suddenly a servant of God—had come to Jerusalem. He finds himself in the crowd. Then he's in the midst of the drama, suddenly confronted with a cross moment.

The Romans call him out, and he must respond to help Jesus the man fulfill his mission to become Jesus, the Savior of the world.

Today the Savior Jesus calls you out of the crowd into the center of the drama of daily life, into your own cross moment. When you proclaim him "Lord" he moves you off the edge of life to center your life around saving activities—saving an abandoned motorist, saving a needy neighbor, saving a faith-challenged friend.

Jesus calls you to pick up your cross to crucify the sin that keeps you from him. He calls you, also, to help others bear their cross that they may crucify their sins, bury their guilt, rise into true life and ascend to heaven's truths.

Simon's life on earth changed in a cross moment. What is the result? Note the reference to his sons Rufus and Alexander. In *Acts 19:33* you see Alexander attempting to quell an assembly against Christianity and in *Romans 16:13 Greet Rufus, chosen in the Lord.*

It seems Simon's cross moment changed his family's life forever.

Pause and consider cross moments are life-changing moments.

They Crucified Him

> Mark 15:22-24 They brought Jesus to the place called Golgotha (which means The Place of the Skull). 23 Then they offered him wine mixed with myrrh, but he did not take it. 24 And they crucified him. Dividing up his clothes, they cast lots to see what each would get.

ONE simple sentence, "And they crucified him." Here is the moment God promised as he speaks to Satan in *Genesis 3:15 "And I will put enmity between you and the woman, and between your offspring and hers; he will crush your head, and you will strike his heel."* Satan has struck "his heel". The forces of sin are physically killing the Son of God made flesh in Jesus.

Yet, this is critical to your salvation. "And they crucified him." is a necessary step in the Father's plan to save your soul as all history moved to Jesus' crucifixion.

As a result, you praise God for the second part of the Genesis promise: *"He will crush your head."* Through the crucifixion will come Jesus' resurrection and his ascension to Heaven's throne. From his throne, Jesus sends the Holy Spirit to crush the head of evil destroying the world. The Spirit has changed countless hearts to Jesus' salvation as he crushes sin's death and raises hearts to Jesus' life. Behold the victory promise!

Revelation 21:7-9 *"He who overcomes will inherit all this, and I will be his God and he will be my son. 8 But the cowardly, the unbelieving, the vile, the murderers, the sexually immoral, those who practice magic arts, the idolaters and all liars — their place will be in the fiery lake of burning sulfur. This is the second death."*

Praise God! Because of "*And they crucified him.*" You can live.

Pause and consider: is sin crushed in you?

A Good Place to Be

Killing the King

> *Mark 15:25-26 It was the third hour when they crucified him. 26 The written notice of the charge against him read: THE KING OF THE JEWS.*

WHEN was Jesus on the cross? Why was Jesus on the cross? Two questions I'll answer for you.

When Mark says 'the third hour" Mark refers to the Jewish day segmented into 4 parts: first at sunrise, the second about 9 am, the third at noon and the fourth at 3 pm. The "third hour" refers to the beginning of the third segment. Thus, Jesus was crucified at noon.

Why was Jesus crucified? Under God's will, of course, his death atoned for mankind's sins. But the political and religious reason was his claim to be the King of the Jews. In the multiple trials that morning, Jesus affirmed the "king charge". (*Mark 15:2 "Are you the king of the Jews?" asked Pilate. "Yes, it is as you say," Jesus replied.*) And although the priests accused Jesus of many things before Pilate, this king charge was the one charge Pilate could use to condemn Jesus. If Rome viewed Jesus as a rebel claiming his kingship over Israel, he would be an enemy of the state, a crime punishable by crucifixion. This is, in fact, the only reason Rome in principle crucified people. Pilate creates the sign to point to Rome as the Jews' true authority. He also is likely warning any "wanna-be messiahs" to dare not challenge Rome.

Of course, the life-giving truth you can see here is that Jesus, indeed, was then and is now the King of the Jews. He humbly submitted himself to the cross for you.

Pause and consider how you must hail the King.

Find Jesus Follow Jesus

God's "Unfair" Act

> Mark 15:27-30 *They crucified two robbers with him, one on his right and one on his left. 29 Those who passed by hurled insults at him, shaking their heads and saying, "So! You who are going to destroy the temple and build it in three days, 30 come down from the cross and save yourself!"*

PILATE had released, in place of Jesus, Barabbas, one sentenced to death for insurrection. Evidence shows these two robbers flanking Jesus were Barabbas' co-conspirators. "Robbers" means "revolutionaries". Barabbas was likely scheduled to be crucified with these two men (Their names were Zoathan {right hand} and Chamnmatha).

Luke records a conversation between Jesus and the two. One mocked Jesus and condemned Jesus for not physically saving him. The other defended Jesus, repenting of his guilt. Jesus responded to the repentant robber (*Luke 23:43 Jesus answered him, "I tell you the truth, today you will be with me in paradise."*)

Now think about this. God had acted to save this man on this day, didn't he? If Pilate had released Jesus instead of Barabbas, this robber would not have met Jesus. He would have had no desire to repent of his sins. And he certainly would have entered into Hell on that day, crucified as a sinner. Instead, this robber became the first human saved from Hell in the atoning death of Jesus.

When we read of Pilate releasing Barabbas, the killer, and crucifying Jesus, the Savior, we often think, "Stupid Pilate! You released the wrong guy!" But the truth is he released, in God's plan, the right guy and crucified the Son of Man to save the robber and to save you. What a remarkable love God has for you.

Pause and consider: are you joyful God "unfairly" sacrificed Jesus for you?

A Good Place to Be

Need Rebuilding?

> Mark 15:29-32 *Those who passed by hurled insults at him, shaking their heads and saying, "So! You who are going to destroy the temple and build it in three days, 30 come down from the cross and save yourself!" 31 In the same way the chief priests and the teachers of the law mocked him among themselves. "He saved others," they said, "but he can't save himself! 32 Let this Christ, this King of Israel, come down now from the cross, that we may see and believe." Those crucified with him also heaped insults on him.*

THE crucifiers weren't satisfied to only nail Jesus to the wood. Drive nails into a man's hands and feet, then stand back to insult and mock him. Sin is a cruel destroyer, isn't it?

The thing is, these mockers thought they were right. They heard Jesus say he'd destroy the temple and rebuild it in 3 days. They didn't understand he meant his own body. They mocked Jesus because to them his claims were meaningless. They thought he had spoken of earthly things, and he had no power to change anything.

Little did they know Jesus had spoken eternal truth. As his body the temple was rebuilt, Jesus is now empowered to rebuild you.

Jesus came to rebuild people's lives then and your life now out the brokenness you are experiencing. Is it the brokenness of worry, fear of work tomorrow, uncertainty in a relationship, separation from a loved one…and the list goes on. Regardless of your brokenness, look to Jesus' power for you. Refrain from mocking him with your disinterest and disbelief. Believe his words. See him from your heart. Know his words are eternally, powerfully rebuilding for you.

Pause and consider Jesus' power builds you anew.

Find Jesus Follow Jesus

Abandoned

> Mark 15:33-34 *At the sixth hour darkness came over the whole land until the ninth hour. 34 And at the ninth hour Jesus cried out in a loud voice, "Eloi, Eloi, lama sabachthani?"-which means, "My God, my God, why have you forsaken me?"*

JESUS' cry from the cross rings loud and tragic through the ages. "Why, my Jehovah, the One who is Eternal, Deliverer, why have you abandoned me, your Son?"

Alone in agony on the cross, the Son of Man cries out, and he seeks an answer you and I often need to know. "Why have you abandoned me, God? Have you left me to die? Have you allowed my enemies to triumph? Why, God, have you not saved me? You promised you would always be my God. Why am I all alone?"

Sometimes the answer comes. Sometimes there is no answer. The question lingers until the day God returns to you. You see that in David's life story. You see that in Job's story. You see that in Jonah's story. You see it in Daniel's story. You see it in all the stories of the Bible as God transforms his world and his people to his salvation. Certainly, you see it in Jesus' story.

God had left his son to die on a cross, but he had not abandoned Jesus forever. As Jesus cried out, his human agony was deep in his soul, his human pain was excruciating to his body; yet, the day came when his Father returned to him to restore his life.

Do you feel God has abandoned you? Jesus knows your feeling. He also knows the joy of reuniting with the Father. Stay with Jesus, and he'll lead you home to the Father, too.

Pause and consider Jesus is your way to life. He is.

A Good Place to Be

Any Hope?

> Mark 15:35-37 *When some of those standing near heard this, they said, "Listen, he's calling Elijah." 36 One man ran, filled a sponge with wine vinegar, put it on a stick, and offered it to Jesus to drink. "Now leave him alone. Let's see if Elijah comes to take him down," he said. 37 With a loud cry, Jesus breathed his last.*

I ALWAYS marvel at this last moment of Jesus' earthly life because of the last strain of hope some at the cross seem to exhibit. As Jesus cried out, (Mark 15:34) *"My God, my God, why have you forsaken me?"* some seemed to believe God might answer his cry and send the prophet Elijah, who had lived some 8 centuries earlier. Why would they think that?

The scriptures declare in *Malachi 4:5 "See, I will send you the prophet Elijah before that great and dreadful day of the Lord comes."* Devout Jews expected Elijah, who had entered heaven on a whirlwind (*2 Kings 2:11*), would return in glory and power ahead of the Messiah to establish God's rule on earth. As Jesus called out to God, the bystanders might have hoped, "What if Elijah comes and Jesus is the Messiah? We must be ready." As they offered to Jesus some meager relief, do you think they were "covering their bases" in the event Elijah did come to Jesus' rescue?

I wonder who they were…some of Jesus' accusers…some of Jesus' disciples? Were they men who hoped in Jesus and clung to a final thread of hope in Jesus' plea?

Too often we live standing by the cross, not sure if we want to commit to the Messiah. But we must. That is the only way you will be ready for the *"great and dreadful day of the Lord"*.

Pause and consider your Messiah.

Find Jesus Follow Jesus

Torn Open

> Mark 15:38-39 *The curtain of the temple was torn in two from top to bottom. 39 And when the centurion, who stood there in front of Jesus, heard his cry and saw how he died, he said, "Surely this man was the Son of God!"*

GOD created a most sacred place inside his temple called the "Holy of Holies". The Lord's priests of the temple could only enter into this sanctuary, symbolizing a personal presence with God, one day a year. Here one priest would make atonement, sacrificing for the sins of the Jews. To be in God's presence was a privileged, sacred, and fearful moment that required very specific acts of repentance before the priest entered.

The Law of Moses was a system God established to teach his people of his holiness. He required them to approach him in a specific way of sacrifices, festivals and worship, so they would understand they were dealing with the "holy of holy" God, the Righteous One who had no sin.

Now, God has sacrificed his Son. At Jesus' death, the holy God tore the Holy of Holies curtain to demonstrate to the Jews the final sacrifice had been offered. God made a new promise with his people that day and said in effect, "My Son's death will tear the curtain of sin from your heart when you confess your sin and Jesus as your Lord."

When the centurion said, *"Surely this man was the Son of God!"* he may have been the first to receive this new promise called the New Testament. On this day, the centurion recognizes Jesus as God's son. God's New Testament is beginning to work in him and into the world it will unceasingly go.

Pause and consider: is sin's veil torn from your heart?

A Good Place to Be

Devotion

> Mark 15:40-47 Some women were watching from a distance. Among them were Mary Magdalene, Mary the mother of James the younger and of Joses, and Salome. 41 In Galilee these women had followed him and cared for his needs. Many other women who had come up with him to Jerusalem were also there. 42 It was Preparation Day (that is, the day before the Sabbath). So as evening approached, 43 Joseph of Arimathea, a prominent member of the Council, who was himself waiting for the kingdom of God, went boldly to Pilate and asked for Jesus' body. 44 Pilate was surprised to hear that he was already dead. Summoning the centurion, he asked him if Jesus had already died. 45 When he learned from the centurion that it was so, he gave the body to Joseph. 46 So Joseph bought some linen cloth, took down the body, wrapped it in the linen, and placed it in a tomb cut out of rock. Then he rolled a stone against the entrance of the tomb. 47 Mary Magdalene and Mary the mother of Joses saw where he was laid

ARE YOU devoted to Jesus? Do you honor him with your actions? Are you loyal to him in your love? Do you support him with your words? Do you commit to him in your worship?

If you're not sure how to answer these questions, perhaps look at the people in this scripture. The women listed here had been committed and loyal to Jesus throughout his ministry. Now, in spite of the danger of association with him, they commit to him as he dies on the cross, and they go even to the tomb. Amid the death and danger their devotion would lead them to life.

Pause and consider how far you are willing to devote your life to Jesus.

Find Jesus Follow Jesus

Hope's Here

> Mark 16:1-4 *When the Sabbath was over, Mary Magdalene, Mary the mother of James, and Salome bought spices so that they might go to anoint Jesus' body. 2 Very early on the first day of the week, just after sunrise, they were on their way to the tomb 3 and they asked each other, "Who will roll the stone away from the entrance of the tomb?" 4 But when they looked up, they saw that the stone, which was very large, had been rolled away.*

HOW much energy do you waste on fear? How often has fear kept you from reaching your goals or fulfilling your God-given potential?

Since Jesus' death and burial, the women had waited for this morning, so they could devotedly care for Jesus' body in the tomb. It appears, though, they had to deal with a particular fear, *"Who will roll the stone away from the entrance of the tomb?"*

The women were committed to caring for Jesus' body; yet, they were afraid they couldn't complete their task. They were afraid he stone was too big. They were afraid no one would help them.

But notice, they didn't let their fear keep them from their task. Devoted to their cause, the women looked past their fear and focused on their hope that someone to roll away the stone.

Have you ever noticed how fear diminishes when you focus on hope? The women's hope was sufficient to lead them to their task. The Lord was sufficient to make their hope a reality and roll away the stone.

Step forward in hope, and you will see God's power in your life. Put your hope in the Lord, and seemingly immovable fears will roll away.

Pause and consider fears go when hope In Jesus grows.

A Good Place to Be

He's Not Here

> *Mark 16:5-8 As they entered the tomb, they saw a young man dressed in a white robe sitting on the right side, and they were alarmed. 6 "Don't be alarmed," he said. "You are looking for Jesus the Nazarene, who was crucified. He has risen! He is not here. See the place where they laid him. 7 But go, tell his disciples and Peter, 'He is going ahead of you into Galilee. There you will see him, just as he told you.'" 8 Trembling and bewildered, the women went out and fled from the tomb. They said nothing to anyone, because they were afraid.*

FEAR keeps challenging you. There's always another challenge to your hope. Sometimes reality is so inexplicable, fear is your only response. The stone is rolled away, but Jesus is gone! What's more this man said, *"He is risen! You'll see him in Galilee."* Why are the women trembling and afraid? The words were abrupt. They made no sense. Instead of powerful and life-changing they were fearfully received.

Could it be they didn't fully or really believe the angel's words? What would happen if they were true? Everything would change, wouldn't it? Their understanding of Jesus would change. Their belief in God would change. Jesus' resurrection is a life-altering event. Life-altering is fearful.

Could that be why it's so hard to really believe in Jesus' resurrection? To know the Living Lord will dramatically change your life can be a fearful thing. You're not sure what change will do. You prefer to stay with what you know. Fearfully you run from the Good News, "He is not here."

No, he's not in the tomb. Turn and meet your Living Lord. Let him alter your life.

Pause and consider how real is Jesus' resurrection for you?

Find Jesus Follow Jesus

Doubt

> Mark 16:9-11 When Jesus rose early on the first day of the week, he appeared first to Mary Magdalene, out of whom he had driven seven demons. 10 She went and told those who had been with him and who were mourning and weeping. 11 When they heard that Jesus was alive and that she had seen him, they did not believe it.

"**DOUBT**" is a negative word to use as we devote some time to our risen Lord. But doubt can be around, can't it, in those fleeting moments when you wonder, "Is Jesus all who the Scriptures say he is?"

I am sure he is. My doubt left years ago. I faithfully believe with all my heart, mind and soul in my risen Savior. But I do not say that boastfully. I say that gratefully, knowing it is only in God's grace he has revealed that truth to me.

Do you have doubt? I hope you read this as a loving question. Mary told the disciples, "Jesus is risen!" but they did not believe her. What would it take for them to, without a doubt, faithfully know in their heart, mind and soul that Jesus is their risen Savior?

There would have to be a moment when each person knew the truth for himself. In God's grace, the Holy Spirit would need to remove the doubt and give to them a true understanding of Jesus.

So as you answer my question, "Do you have doubt?" I'd like you to consider if you've had that moment of knowing, "Jesus is my Lord." Do you live free of doubt regarding that truth? If the doubt's still around, keep seeking Jesus. Pray for the Spirit's power to reveal the risen Savior to you. Pray the Spirit removes all doubt.

Pause and consider a doubt-free life.

A Good Place to Be

He Sent Them Anyway

> Mark 16:12-20 *Afterward Jesus appeared in a different form to two of them while they were walking in the country. 13 These returned and reported it to the rest; but they did not believe them either. 14 Later Jesus appeared to the Eleven as they were eating; he rebuked them for their lack of faith and their stubborn refusal to believe those who had seen him after he had risen. 15 He said to them, "Go into all the world and preach the good news to all creation. 16 Whoever believes and is baptized will be saved, but whoever does not believe will be condemned. 17 And these signs will accompany those who believe: In my name they will drive out demons; they will speak in new tongues; 18 they will pick up snakes with their hands; and when they drink deadly poison, it will not hurt them at all; they will place their hands on sick people, and they will get well." 19 After the Lord Jesus had spoken to them, he was taken up into heaven and he sat at the right hand of God. 20 Then the disciples went out and preached everywhere, and the Lord worked with them and confirmed his word by the signs that accompanied it.*

CHRIST'S followers today have a problem: We think we have to be "perfect", have to have it "all together" before we can do Jesus' work. Time and again I'll ask people to do something in the church, and they will say, "I don't do that."

Guess what. I know you don't do that. But I feel God has lead me to ask you. When you say, "No." are you saying, "No." to Jesus?

The disciples could have said, "I don't do that." None of them had the kind of "church experience" to do Jesus' work. Worse, *"he rebuked them for their lack of faith and their stubborn refusal to believe those who had seen him after he had risen."* Jesus' own disciples had refused the message of his resurrection!

But Jesus sent them anyway. Through his Spirit *"the Lord worked with them and confirmed his word by the signs that accompanied it."* Jesus mentored his disciples from Heaven's throne. Through the Holy Spirit, he qualified them day by day. Through these unqualified men, Jesus began his church, and his church grew.

How do you do Jesus' work on earth? It's not about you, what you like to do, what qualifies you. It's about Jesus. No one is qualified without Jesus. Nothing will be accomplished without Jesus. When you obey the Lord of Hosts, he will send the Spirit to work with you and through you. In the power of Jesus, God's will is done on earth.

Pause and consider what Jesus is calling you to do. Are you calling on him to be with you?

A Good Place to Be

WE began this walk with Jesus with a blessing from Jude near the end of the Bible. I leave you with this blessing from Numbers, the 4th book of the Bible. God is a God of blessing. He has given you himself. Now bless him back with your praise to him. Bless others in his name.

Numbers 6:24-27
24 """The Lord bless you
and keep you;
25 the Lord make his face shine upon you
and be gracious to you;
26 the Lord turn his face toward you
and give you peace." '
27 "So they will put my name on the Israelites,
and I will bless them."